DARK MAGUS

DARK MAGUS

The Jekyll and Hyde
Life of Miles Davis

As Narrated by His Son
Gregory Davis
with **Les Sussman**

"It was thus rather the exacting nature of my aspirations, than any
particular degradation in my faults, that made me what I was...."
—*Dr. Henry Jekyll's Full Statement of the Case*

**Backbeat
Books**
San Francisco

Published by Backbeat Books
600 Harrison Street, San Francisco, CA 94107
www.backbeatbooks.com
email: books@musicplayer.com

CMP
United Business Media

A CMP Information company

Distributed to the book trade in the US and Canada by
Publishers Group West, 1700 Fourth Street, Berkeley, CA 94710

Distributed to the music trade in the US and Canada by
Hal Leonard Publishing, P.O. Box 13819, Milwaukee, WI 53213

Cover design by Richard Leeds — BigWigDesign.com
Front cover photo © Luciano Vito/RETNA Ltd.
Author's photo © Christo Holloway/Clockwork Apple
Composition by Dovetail Publishing Services

Library of Congress Cataloging-in-Publication Data

Davis, Gregory.
Dark magus : the Jekyll and Hyde life of Miles Davis / as narrated by his son
Gregory Davis, with Les Sussman.
    p. cm.
  Includes index.
  ISBN-13: 978-0-87930-875-9 (alk. paper)
  ISBN-10: 0-87930-875-3 (alk. paper)
1. Davis, Miles. 2. Jazz musicians--United States--Biography. I. Sussman,
Les, 1944- II. Title.

ML419.D39D38 2006
788.9'2165092--dc22
  [B]
                                2006027501

Printed in the United States of America

06 07 08 09 10   5 4 3 2 1

DEDICATION

To Dr. Miles Dewey Davis, my grandfather,

who was a dedicated family man with exemplary

principles and a role model of what African-Americans

can accomplish against all odds.

Contents

Foreword

By Clark Terry

MILES WASN'T A SAINT. I can tell you that much because I knew him for a long, long time. But he was also a great man and I miss him very much.

I remember the time when he was sick and I found him laying in the gutter like a bum on 52nd and Broadway. I picked him up from the sidewalk and brought him into one of those ham and eggers and bought him some ham and eggs. Then I took him back to my hotel on 47th Street.

I said, "Hey, Miles, get some sleep and I'll be back in a couple of hours. I'll bring you some tea or sandwiches or something."

When I got back a couple of hours later my door was open. I rushed into the room—no Miles. No radio. No furniture. No clothes that I had just bought. Miles had taken all that and absconded with it. Then, to top it off, the next day I saw a good friend of mine traipsing down Broadway wearing the brand-new shirt I had just bought.

Well, you gotta forgive old friends for their weaknesses, and Miles and I went back a long time together. What I remember most about him is that as a young and upcoming musician he was very shy and very timid. He was very unsure of himself—so much so that he sometimes had problems looking you in the eye. He would look down on the ground, and a lot of people took that the wrong way.

I also remember that he was so thin that his wife, Irene, once told me that if he stood sideways they would mark him absent. But aside from that he was always a studious kind of player.

Miles came into my life way back when. I remember that Elwood Buchanan, who was a friend of mine and went to school in East St. Louis with him, used to tell me, "You gotta come over to the school and hear this dude Davis, play."

I lived in St. Louis at the time so I went over and met him. He looked down all the time he talked to me—that's how shy he was. Then one day he came down to Carbondale, Illinois, where I was working with a band. They were having what was called a "scholastic maypole winding."

They had lots of pretty girls that came down to wind the maypole, and I was hired to play in the band for the kids. So I saw Miles for the second time. He came up to me and started asking me questions about playing trumpet. I said, "Hey, man, I don't want to talk about no damn trumpet playing now. I want to look at all these girls doing the maypole winding."

The third time I saw him was in a place called the Elks Lodge on Cardinal Street in St. Louis. This was in a loft way up on a long flight of stairs. This was where all the cats used to hang out and play dance sessions.

One particular night I went there when Eddie Rabbit and his band was playing. I went into the building to see the band and I heard this trumpet. There must have been about 90 steps to get up to the top of the stairs, and I'm listening to this great trumpet being played; it was so full of soul.

When I got to the top and waltzed into the room, there was Miles playing in Eddie Rabbit's band. So I said to him, "Hey, man, aren't you the cat who—," and he interrupted me and finished the sentence. "Yeah, I'm the cat you fluffed off in Carbondale."

After that, we became lifelong friends. And as I already said, he wasn't a saint. He was very bitter because he didn't have any hardships when he was raised—his father was a successful dentist—and he never had to take any crap from anybody.

So when he came out to the world and started playing, well, sometimes things got tough for him. But he still didn't like to take any crap from anybody—and he didn't. And that's when he was far from a saint.

Over the years, I mostly always thought of him as a fantastic person. He was very encouraging and very inspiring to younger players who came to him because of his talent.

I'm glad Gregory now has a chance to tell us more about his father than anyone else ever has. He was Miles's son and was with him a lot. He was also with me a lot back in the early days.

Back when we all lived at this hotel on 47th Street, Irene and Gregory were home a lot because Miles was kind of lifted off on narcotics at that time. So I actually used to baby-sit for him. He was like my son, and he felt like I was his father. But I was his godfather. As a matter of fact, we hung out so much together that people got to thinking that he was my son. He didn't even know Irene as well as he knew me.

This book brings back many memories to me about Miles—some good and some not so good. I still miss him very much. We were close to the very end, even when he was dying in a hospital in California and I was sick in a hospital in New York City. I used to call him two or three times a week.

The last thing I remember Miles telling me was, "We're gonna knock these motherfuckers out so we can both be champions." I didn't know if he was talking about our illnesses or what, but it typified Miles, who was always a champion as far as I was concerned.

Introduction

YOU OFTEN HEAR ABOUT BOOKS that were a long time in the making. Due to the controversial, sometimes painful, and often bizarre relationship I had with my father, this is one of them.

It wasn't delayed by length of labor, but rather my reluctance to write it at all. I found it difficult to intentionally strip away my father's cool image and to relive and publicly narrate the traumatic relationship I had with him. In short, this was not an easy memoir to write.

As his son, I lived with Miles longer than any other family member. I laughed and cried with and for him, nursed and cared for him when no one else would or could, and was with my father during many of his finest moments as well as many of his most notorious escapades.

That's why the hardest part of writing this book was presenting my father objectively from a subjective viewpoint, without taking the tone or intention of a "Daddy Dearest" type of memoir.

But after finally making the decision to put his story on paper, I wanted to make sure I presented Miles in a larger, more accurate and personal way than any of the other books, articles, and media features that have been done on him over the years.

In researching much of those materials, what I discovered is that despite the volume of accounts reporting Miles's life and career, it seems no one who actually knew him from the inside had ever written anything definitive about him—that is, both sides of my father: the good and bad, the Dr. Jekyll and Mr. Hyde of him. I wanted this book to be totally Miles!

Most of my family and close friends agree that there's a lot of Miles that isn't there in books about him—mostly just snatches and pieces of the man, but nothing that really revealed the inside of such an outside man. Even the best-selling book about my father to date—Quincy Troupe's *Miles: The Autobiography*—failed to portray the heart and soul of my father.

Many of my family members, my closest friends, and myself are still irritated by the many inaccuracies and unlikely episodes found in books that were reportedly narrated by my father. Most of us feel that much of the writing about Miles stems from the fertile imaginations of the authors.

I'll never forget how annoyed Miles was in reading Quincy Troupe's book, claiming that a lot of it was taken out of context. He told me on several occasions that he couldn't remember saying this or that.

But in all fairness to Mr. Troupe, it was a well-written book and did cover the general gist of my father's career. I now think that if Miles did, in fact, tell Mr. Troupe all those contradictory tales, then it was obvious that he couldn't even be trusted to tell the truth about himself.

Most of the published pieces written about my father over the years are just plain bullshit—more of who my father wasn't than who he was. Miles loved that persona, though. He very often found the fictionalized accounts of his deeds far more interesting than the factual accounts.

Sometimes when he read an article or story about something that he was alleged to have said or done, he'd get a kick out of it. He would break up laughing and just shake his head. Of course, there were many other times he didn't find what was written about him all that funny.

But one thing for sure: He never lacked for people eager to become media parties to his myths. Miles got a kick out of putting people on, creating the various mystiques that amused him and fascinated them.

So, perhaps, I can't always fault the pundits for their conflicting accounts of his remarkable career and eccentric personality, since he, himself, was often the source of the scuttlebutt and notoriety with which he has become labeled.

It was at the urging of my mother—with her help and that of other family members and close friends who know more truthful and complete versions of my father's story—that I decided to set the record straight and rat out the real Miles.

I know it's virtually impossible for any person to be privy to the perfect analysis and appreciation of any other human being, their relationships or true intentions—even between spouse, parent, child, or close confidants.

No one will ever get it totally right; there will always be elements of supposition and interpretation. But I do believe this book—my version of who, what, how, and why he was—is the best version of my father that the reader will ever get.

Ironically, among the many bizarre facts and facets associated with the Miles Davis mystique, in more than a few cases what actually happened was at least as intriguing as the fiction. In this book I hope to bring people closer to the real Miles—show what he was really like when he wasn't imitating who he was supposed to be.

I have neither glorified nor demeaned him here. I've tried to honestly show both his best side and his darkest side. Hopefully, this account will present a truer picture of a larger-than-life individual: a complex yet simplistic man with enviable strengths and talents, but also with overwhelming human frailties.

My father was an extraordinary man-child who, despite his flawed personal behavior and incredibly negative social attitudes, became one of the most important and influential cultural lights in the evolution and propagation of African-American classical music.

Miles was a man who inspired an international community of music lovers to appreciate, emulate, and even to revere him. Yet his genius never equipped him to develop the personal, familial, and social skills that most of us take for granted.

In this book I want to introduce to readers the man and the effect that he left indelibly imprinted on his family and the world. This is the Miles that his thousands of fans around the world have yet to meet, not just another chronicle of his life and career. There are already plenty of histories out there on the man.

I bring no sour grapes to this book, a minimum of emotional baggage, and the desire not to taint the recollection of my father with my own crap! I want this book to reflect the way one of my close friends—the late Nizam Fatah—saw Miles: down to earth, in the nitty gritty, with nothing but his drawers on.

Gregory Davis
New York City, 2006

CHAPTER ONE

Old Folks
(Columbia, 1961)

From Slavery to Success

THE DAVIS FAMILY'S ROOTS in this country can be clearly traced to my great-grandfather's plantation life in Noble Lake, Arkansas. From the things my father told me that his father told him, we were somewhat successful with our White masters: Despite our dark skin, somehow we managed to become "house Niggas," deemed to have unusual intelligence and cultural abilities for Negroes.

Still, in spite of our enslavement and forced servitude, even in the alien and hostile environment of early America, we managed to retain a healthy consciousness of our Black heritage, always challenging our own innate ability to struggle and stay alive with some measure of dignity.

In addition to performing our mandatory chores, it also fell upon our family to master and perform various aspects of European classical music, which we were often required to present at many of the plantation's social and political functions.

They say our family's strong sense of character, self-esteem, and cultural talents seemed to amuse the "mastahs." Now, don't get me wrong! The Davis clan was never "good Niggas" or "Super Toms" in any way.

But our wit, survival skills, and cultural talents kept the White folks at bay. My father said that our family entertained them just enough to keep from suffering the fates of Kunta Kinte and Chicken George.

My father's grandfather was named Miles Dewey Davis. He was the first of us to carry that name. He was a serious rebel and smart as well. He was not only a hellafied musician, but also managed to become an accomplished man of letters and numbers—no mean feat for a Black man of that day and time.

When slavery was said to be abolished by the Emancipation Proclamation, he managed to do better than most. He could read and write, and he even earned a pretty good living as an accountant, primarily for White folks. But he was still a "Nigga" and required to stay in a "Nigga's" place—that of obedience and subjugation; rarely seen and never heard, out of sight and out of mind.

Yet, even in that shadow role his presence became too strong—too pronounced. So it wasn't long before he fell into disfavor with the powers that controlled the climate at the time.

A lot of it had to do with the fact that he had purchased a large tract of prime land from one of his accounting clients, and many of the White folks in that part of the country took exception to that.

My great-grandfather was thought to be a bit too mannish for a "Nigga," so they took steps to make sure that land didn't stay in his hands. Shortly afterwards, "circumstances" forced our family to relocate to Alton, Illinois. It was there that he set up the first real housekeeping for himself and the Davis family.

My Grandpa Was a Mean Mooterscooter

Miles Dewey Davis, Jr., who to this day I still refer to as Dr. Davis due to his strong paternal presence, dignity, and professional accomplishments, was among the first African-American dentists. At age 27 he graduated from Northwestern University with his D.D.S. degree.

From what my mother and other relatives tell me, in many ways he was like my great-grandfather—a mean motorscooter, a no-nonsense kind of guy obsessed with being all that he could be, on his own terms.

By the time Grandpa began to set up his own household, Great-Grandpa had gone back to Arkansas to homestead, farm, and landlord his property. Around that time Grandpa married Cleo Henry, my grandmother, who we always called "Mama-Cleo."

She was an educated woman but tough as nails. Grammar fanatic, eloquent speaker, obsessed with good diction and proper enunciation, Grandma was always correcting somebody on this or that syntax: You could do no "uh-huh," "un-huh," nod, or shake your head with Mama-Cleo. You had to "open your mouth when you talk, boy!"

My father and Uncle Vernon were her pet projects—especially Miles. One of the things I remember about my grandparents was that they were both into style. They were serious fashion plates. They loved clothes and were always elegant and *en vogue*. It seemed like they were always dressed up, even when they weren't going anywhere. I think that's where my father's lifelong love for clothes and fashion came from.

Tough Love

My father was born Miles Dewey Davis III on May 26, 1926, in Alton, Illinois. Like me, he was the first son, born between an older sister—Cheryl Ann— and younger brother Vernon.

Eventually, we all wound up in East St. Louis, Illinois, a small town on the Mississippi River.

After establishing himself in his profession, Grandpa moved us into a grand house on the corner of 1701 Kansas. Due to its size, I guess it could be called a mansion.

The Davises have lived in that house going on three-quarters of a century. Uncle Vernon, my father's baby brother, a hellafied musician in his own right as well as a composer and vocalist who is very well known in the gospel music field, lived there until his death a few years ago.

I remember Mama-Cleo telling us about an incident that involved her, Dr. Davis, and that house. The way she told it, one day some White folks came to our house and she answered the door, looking gorgeous and well groomed as always.

It was a couple trying to find a house on our block that had been put up for sale. Before Grandma could give any directions, Grandpa came to the door. He was also impeccably dressed. He directed the couple to the people whose property was up for sale.

As the story goes, when the White couple finally found the people who were selling the house (who were also White), the prospective female buyer confided to the selling family: "Would you believe some smart-assed Nigga servants in the big house on the corner answered the door and directed us here without conferring with their master about speaking directly to decent high-bred White people? If we take this house, the first thing we'll do is horsewhip them and teach them some manners."

The White family selling the house had been neighbors for many years. They knew Dr. Davis and our family very well. They replied, "Oh, those are the Davises. They're not really Niggas in the Nigga sense. He's a doctor—a real dentist—he graduated from Northwestern. They own that house on the corner, some hog farms, and quite a few other properties around here."

I never did hear the follow-up to find out whether those people ever became our neighbors. But I guess not, because Mama-Cleo never mentioned anything about a horsewhipping in our family!

I guess that couple would really have lost it had they known that there were several other prominent Black home owners on that block. Can you imagine what they would have thought this world was coming to?

Mama-Cleo told us that story more than once. We always knew that at least part of it was meant to pull our coats and alert us to the reality of racism—prepare us to keep our eyes on the prize and our souls in the right place. But as concerned as Grandma was about prejudice and bigotry, Grandpa was almost psychotic.

He had disdain and distrust for nearly all White folks and everything they represented. He was very activist and political, and every day he had another bone to pick.

It was very important to him that we knew as African-Americans that no matter who or what we became, we should remain conscious of racism in all its forms, be prepared to confront it, and take a principled and aggressive stand against it at all times.

My grandparents would have turned over in their graves had Miles—or any of us for that matter—become a Clarence Thomas, Diana Ross, Whoopi Goldberg, or Tiger Woods, pretending that we were exempted from racism, believing that we had become successful enough to become an honorary White.

The Davises have always been a proud people, trying to hold our heads up, never hunching our shoulders, knowing our geography—where we came from, where we were at, and where we wanted to go. Grandpa and Grandma taught my father to stand his own ground, and always be who and what he was—that as black as his ass was, it was still beautiful.

I think our parental structure was typical of most Black families at that time. The men were in charge and the women, for the most part, let them think so. The fathers in my family were never particularly nice guys to their sons; they weren't the kiss, hug, and hold your hand types, and Miles followed that pattern.

Nothing cruel, nothing really physically abusive—just everything was done with an iron hand. It's not that they wouldn't kick your ass for doing something wrong, it's just that they pretty much left what many people call *corporal punishment* to the mothers.

Our fathers were more into the diabolical punishments of browbeating and character assassination in response to insolence, acting ugly, or getting beside ourselves. Whatever the case, with them it was always tough love; everything in our lives had to be a lesson. On the male side of my family, it was understood that this was the only way you could become a man.

I Never Want to Be the Type of Father Miles Was

I grew up hearing how strict my great-grandfather was on Dr. Davis, and in turn I saw firsthand how tough Dr. Davis could be on Miles and Vernon. Only after they became grandfathers themselves did they soften up and become to their grandchildren what they never were as fathers.

Miles was definitely a chip off the old block. My father definitely continued that hard-as-nails, drill-instructor tradition with me and my younger brother, Little Miles, who we had nicknamed "Squeaky." But I guess he really didn't know any other way.

People have always told me that Miles, in his own way, was very much like Dr. Davis. And most of our family and friends often tell me how much of Miles they see in me. Maybe so. But I hope there's one trait of his character that I've missed: I never want to be the type of father to my children that he was to me.

The Girls in Our Family Got Off Easy

It was different with the girls in our family. Basically, the Davis guys have always been pretty decent to the females in our immediate circle. We generally spoiled our women. I don't know what happened in my father's case because he could be quite abusive to women.

My mother says he wasn't always the Miles Davis depicted in media accounts reporting his reputed negative romantic relationships and attitudes—fucking over his wives and women, kicking their asses, spitting in their faces, throwing them down stairwells, etc. She always says that even if and when he did at times treat some women badly for whatever reasons, or for no reason at all, Miles sure as hell knew better.

Poitier and Belafonte's Bad Influence Is Not True

When Mama-Cleo first heard rumors about him doing that kind of stuff to women, she wouldn't believe it. "Not Miles," she would say. "The Davises don't act that way." From what family members have told me, all hell broke loose when she found out there was some truth to those rumors.

Grandma, the story goes, really jumped his ass when it came to that subject. She would try to make his life miserable when he was around her. But I already knew way back then that he wasn't exactly a chip off the old block when it came to the treatment of women.

There were times he could be the warmest person in the world—or the coldest. He could be very affectionate or an incredible asshole. The problem for his women was they had no idea which Miles he was going to be at any given time.

I still can remember one supermarket tabloid wrote about him—quoting from "reliable sources"—that his "shut up, bitch" behavior stemmed largely from his association with Sidney Poitier and Harry Belafonte.

The paper claimed those two often acted in the slandering stereotype of Black Caribbean males in regard to their domestic relations with women—you know, whipping some ass anywhere, anytime, for anything.

When I was older and I read that so-called exposé, I had to laugh out loud. I can't recall anything from his association with Sidney or Harry that would ever make me think negatively of them. Although I was pretty young at the time, I remember that they used to hang out around the house.

The thing I knew most about them was that my father really admired and respected them both as friends and artists. I also remember how nice they always were to me.

I mean, I know they weren't angels or anything, and I'm sure they were capable of doing anything any other man is capable of, but as far as I can remember they just seemed to enjoy each other's company. They would talk politics, race relations, sports, listen to music—just general Black man stuff.

In fact, I think if anything they might have been the voices of reason from people he respected—somewhat of a restraining influence on him. I also know that long before Miles ever met either of them, it was not unusual for him to treat other women in his life like shit. I guess when it came to the mistreatment of women, you could say that Miles was a natural.

CHAPTER TWO

The Birth of the Cool
(Capitol-EMI, 1949)

Teen Love

EVERYBODY SAYS THAT EVEN WHEN he was a child most people saw something special about my father. They thought there was something different about him—like he was already Miles Davis, or someday would be.

My mother told me that when she first met Miles in high school—both then in their teens—she felt that this young man was definitely the truth, the real thing. She said it wasn't anything you could put your finger on, because outwardly he was pretty ordinary. But everyone suspected that there was something inside him that could be very important.

But I'll abbreviate a lot of his childhood since I wasn't there. Whatever happened is primarily hearsay to me anyway. Besides, I must admit that Quincy Troupe, in his biography of my father, did a remarkable job of covering his diapers-to-long-pants days.

Shy, Moody, and Often Antisocial

I recall Mama-Cleo once telling me that my father was always somewhat shy and moody, aloof and introspective, but that he was not unapproachable. He had his own handful of people he shared interests with; outside of music, he loved sports, clothes, and cars—in just about that order.

But by the time Miles reached his late teens, he had begun to perfect his antisocial arts. He began to close doors; anybody who wasn't already in his life didn't have much of a chance of getting in.

His brother, Vernon, and my mother were probably the closest people to him, and that's the way my father seemed to like it. But I never knew him to collect friends, anyway. He assessed most folks as "intrusive, exploitive, and/or just plain full of shit."

Miles always said that he had the good sense to be distrustful of people. He said they could be dangerous and, if given the opportunity, most people would go out of their way to hurt, defame, and betray you for no reason at all.

Except for his girlfriends, Miles thought of most people who tried to befriend him as parasites, beggars, bums, or folks without lives of their own hoping to bask in his glory, hit on his wives, squeezes, and groupies.

He was convinced there weren't too many people in the world worth knowing. That was one of the reasons he became so reclusive on- and off-stage. In his last years he hardly dealt with anyone at all.

But without doubt he had particular contempt for most of the people who called themselves *media*. He thought of them as people without virtue or true professions.

To him reporters were "gossip mongers" perpetually looking for something to lie about—"assholes without honor" and "paparazzi fuckfaces" as he not-so-fondly used to call them.

My father used to refer to most of them as "Miles's maggots." I remember him once telling me that most of these writers were no more than street whores who replaced turning tricks with turning in copy.

He said they would move right on to suck off some other artist before they even "wiped the shit off their noses or the cum off their lips." The few journalists he did respect, like Leonard Feather, Barry Ulanov, Boo Frazier, Ralph Gleason, Gene Santoro, and just a couple more generally got pretty decent interviews from him.

A Close Circle of Friends

My father's circle of friends was very tight and damn near inflexible. He always picked his own people and refused to be chosen by others. Yet his people paranoia and poor attitude aside, Miles seemed to have an uncanny sense of good judgment about the people he did choose.

Elwood Buchanan and Clark Terry were among his first and most influential friends, and they remained so throughout his life. When it came to Elwood and Clark, I don't think I ever saw him in a "So What" mode. They were special to him; he respected them as men of music and character.

Elwood Buchanan was well thought of in the East St. Louis area where he grew up. He was a gentleman and a scholar—a real solid citizen. But more importantly to my father, he was also an exceptional musician.

Although Miles started playing trumpet at a pretty early age and truly liked the instrument, it was really Buchanan who inspired him to make music and that horn foremost in his life.

While my father was in the band at Crispus Attucks Junior High, he began taking private trumpet lessons from Elwood. Then he left Attucks to enroll at Lincoln High School where Buchanan was the school's music director.

It was under Elwood's tutelage that my father developed the musicianship and blues/jazz foundation that was at the root of everything great he later produced.

Miles always liked the way Elwood played the horn. His teacher had an almost vibrato-less technique, a middle-register approach, and subtle tone. My father loved that sound and gradually evolved it into the unique and distinctive style that helped make him famous—the Miles Davis trademark: super stingy chord structures, middle-register pitch, spatial phrases, and hanging notes.

My father once remarked that he hung notes in midair because he wanted to teach his notes the same lesson he wanted to teach his children. He said it was his job to make us both learn what we were really there for: to learn to take care of ourselves and make a life of our own.

Grandpa and Grandma Want Miles to Stay Away from Music

Miles's interest in music was not necessarily a priority to my grandparents. They preferred to regard it as more of an extracurricular activity. Although Dr. Davis, himself, truly loved music—as did all the Davis clan—his career agenda for Miles was directed to something more conservative, something with security and economic stability—you know, to be a dentist like him, or a doctor, lawyer, or teacher.

Grandpa was determined to clone my father into the image of himself: a professional man who could achieve some pragmatic success. Miles really tried to relate to his grandpa's career program. He even thought about becoming a doctor. But that goal was always secondary to his love for music.

I think my father knew that his personal objectives weren't all that practical and more than likely not very lucrative either, but he didn't give a damn! He just wanted to play trumpet, play jazz.

The trumpet also created another problem for my father. Brass, reed, and percussion instruments didn't sit too well with Mama-Cleo. My grandmother subscribed to a more delicate cultural scenario. If he were to play anything—even in school—she wanted it to be the violin.

Grandma's choice of instrument for Miles had a lot to do with the fact that she really did love the violin. (She used to play it herself.) It was also based on some well-founded paranoia.

Like many African-American women of her time, she felt violin players weren't so threatening to the masculinity of White musicians or the mainstream social structure, so her son would not place himself in danger. If it had been left to Grandma, Dad would have been another Heifetz or someone tame enough to make her feel less anxious.

I don't think Grandpa gave her anxieties too much thought one way or other. He really didn't care what instrument Miles played prior to his entering some certified professional field. But for the sake of peace in the household, he was inclined to go along with Grandma.

Grandpa Is Persuaded That Miles Can Play

Buchanan and Clark Terry were longtime musician buddies who gigged around town together. And as fate would have it, Dr. Davis often spent his evening hours hanging out with them, socializing, drinking, and just talking the talk.

Grandpa had known Elwood for years and, both being professionals, they shared some of the town's same social circles. I think he met Clark through Elwood. Dr. Davis enjoyed being with them; he could let his hair down and be himself. Prim and proper by day, the three of them could go hog wild at night.

It was during those partying periods that Buchanan began planting the seeds to eventually change Dr. Davis's career plans for Miles and accept music as his son's future. Over drinks, Elwood even got Grandpa to listen to this idea.

But knowing Grandpa, if he had thought such an idea really would come true, he would have balked. To him, my father's interest in music was sort of a good cultural hobby or pastime that might be used as a personal amusement—a minor means to supplement his allowance—like a paper route—or a great way to meet girls. It was something for my father to do while he pursued a real vocation.

Elwood kept telling Grandpa how good Miles played in the school band and in the little groups he played with around town. He would describe all the musical potential that my father had. And, then, to throw Grandpa off the track, he'd mention how it could be used to keep him out of trouble during his college study years.

At that time, Clark Terry had not heard Miles play that much, but he always backed up Elwood: "Aw, Doc, lighten up," Terry would say. "Let the boy see what he can do. Besides, it'll give him a more rounded education—make him a better dentist in the end. It sure as hell can't hurt. It didn't hurt me."

On that last part, Clark, who was super wild in those days—chasing all the girls, drinking it up, dressing like a model from *Esquire*—said everybody at the table had a good laugh.

A Trumpet and a Divorce

With Buchanan and Clark coming at Grandpa from both sides, they finally beat him down. Grandpa told them that "If the boy is getting that good and already playing in front of people and everything, I don't want Junior embarrassing me with that old-assed horn."

On my father's 13th birthday, Dr. Davis secretly presented him with a brand-new trumpet. The deal was that Miles had to keep the trumpet hidden until Grandpa could reconcile the violin-vs.-trumpet issue with Mama-Cleo.

Although Grandma was pissed off, she seemed to come around—at least she stopped rolling her eyes. I later found out that the trumpet incident created some major dissension in our household for quite some time. In fact, when Grandpa and Mama-Cleo got divorced years later, I heard that my father's trumpet was among her complaints.

Clark Terry Becomes a Believer

Clark Terry, who has always been just CT to us, was the man. He was one of the most popular dudes around, known for his wit, his humor, and his skill as a highly regarded amateur boxer. It also goes without saying that nobody around town could touch him on trumpet or otherwise.

Nearly every jazz band that came through St. Louis and southern Illinois was after Clark. CT was one of my father's earliest trumpet influences. Miles always admired his ability to play damn near every kind of jazz. He marveled at his highly stylized technical skills and his mastery in incorporating a dash of humor into the most serious music.

Outside of CT, his primary exposure to other accomplished trumpet players was mostly limited to those he was able to hear on the radio and on popular recordings: It was mostly Harry James, Bobby Hackett, sometimes Louis Armstrong, Buck Clayton, and Roy Eldridge. So having the real live Clark Terry around had meaning.

With Grandpa's birthday gift, Miles became even more of a practice machine—day and night, every spare minute. As Buchanan grew more impressed with my father's musical prowess, he took it upon himself to push and promote Miles in every way he could. He was always telling somebody something about his protégé.

Even though Clark always backed Elwood's advocacy of Miles with Grandpa, he wasn't all that gung ho about my father's talents. On one occasion when Elwood persuaded Clark to come down to hear Miles play at one of the school's music programs, CT's response was "He's okay for a kid, but nothing to write home about."

As Miles kept improving, Buchanan kept the pressure on Clark to give him another listen, but CT always managed to avoid doing so. One night my father went down to a club where Clark was working. When CT got off the stand my father walked over to him, trying to make Clark remember him and let him play some music.

CT kind of brushed him off and moved on to circulate with the rest of the crowd. The story goes that Miles was pissed. He decided from then on he was just going to like CT's trumpet playing but not CT.

About a year and a half later, CT showed up at a club where Miles was playing. By this time my father was beginning to gain an enthusiastic following with his horn-blowing ability.

Even CT was impressed by what he heard and hung around to talk to him. Miles walked over and said, "I was trying to tell you I was a bad muthafucka, but you rounded on me, so don't try to be my friend now." They both cracked up with laughter and were the best of friends ever since.

After that, Clark took my father everywhere. He introduced him to all the bad blowing cats around town, sat in on sessions and played their asses off together. Even though Miles knew he was no match for CT, he sure as hell tried to keep up and even surpass him.

CT got a kick out of that. He told me that he used to look at Miles and think, "This little muthafucka's got balls." Clark taught my father a lot of stuff and added some serious speed to his musical growth. He taught him how to play the flugelhorn and helped him tighten up his technique.

In all the years that followed, whenever my father and CT got together, it was like a ritual. Miles would always remind Clark that he hadn't forgotten being insulted and treated like shit. He would jokingly threaten CT that a payback time would come.

Clark, on his part, would be sitting there looking over the top of his glasses and remind my father that he had been some kind of boxing champion back in those days, and would "whup his little Black ass." Then they'd crack up.

CT was one of the few people my father trusted enough to laugh with. Hardly anyone else he knew made him feel that comfortable. When I was just a few months old, Miles recruited CT as my godfather, and after all these years the same love, concern, and counseling CT always gave to my father he gives to me now.

Miles Davis as a child of nine or ten.

Dr. Miles Dewey Davis, father of Miles Davis and grandfather of Gregory, standing on his land in Millstadt, Illinois.

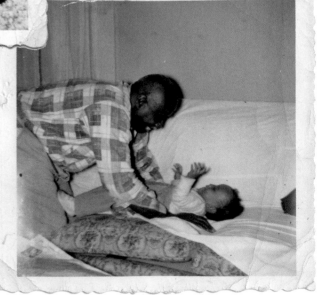

Dr. Miles Dewey Davis playing with Joseph, Miles's half brother.

Miles. Dorothy Mae. Vernon, Mrs.

Miles, his sister Dorothy Mae, Vernon, and his mother, Mrs. Cleo Henry Davis, called "Mama-Cleo."

Cass, Vernon, Johns, Miles

Four boys. Vernon Davis, Miles's brother, is second from left, and Miles is on the right.

Miles and Irene, his first wife and Gregory's mother, outside their high school in East St. Louis where they were high-school sweethearts. Early 1940s.

Irene Davis at her home in University City, Missouri, on Christmas. Early 1980s.

Gregory in uniform in 1966.

Miles Dewey Davis IV, son of
Miles, nicknamed "Squeaky."

Portrait of Miles in front of one of his paintings, New York City, 1969.

Miles and Betty Davis, 1969.

Miles with his Ferrari 275GTB, New York City, 1969.

Miles behind the wheel of his Ferrari. New York City, 1969.

Miles went to Gleason's Gym in New York City to box several times a week, and he compared his style of jazz to his style of boxing.

Miles was always a sharp dresser. At home New in York City, 1972.

Miles performing in the early 1980s in New York City.

Miles at home in Malibu in 1984 or 1985.

Miles Davis's last trumpet, made especially for him right before his death in 1991.

Gregory Davis with friends Peter Bradley and Billy Holloway.

Gregory Davis and Cheryl Davis (at lectern), Miles Davis's son and daughter, accept his induction into the Rock and Roll Hall of Fame onstage at the 21st Annual Hall of Fame induction ceremony at the Waldorf Astoria March 13, 2006, in New York City.

CHAPTER THREE

The Legendary Big Bop Band
(*Billy Eckstine, National, 1946*)

My Mother Thinks She Got Him Started

I CAN'T TELL YOU HOW MANY PEOPLE claim to have the inside track on how, when, and what constituted the origin of my father's professional life. I've heard my mother's version a thousand times, about five different ones from Miles himself, and more than I care to count from jazz historians and many other folks who come out of the woodwork claiming to know everything about him.

My mother claims she was the one to launch him. She always jokes that had she not pushed, pulled, and kind of tricked him into what she regards as his first real public exposure, he might still be sitting around East St. Louis now playing in back of the barbecue shack.

Mother says Miles had been walking around talking big about how good he was getting when she started high jiving him: "Well, if you're so bad and you know Eddie Randle's looking for a trumpet player, how come you ain't down there blowing with the Blue Devils? It's obvious you ain't as good as you say you are since you're too scared to try out for Eddie Randle's band."

My mother told me that Miles got so mad, that he called Eddie Randle asking him for an audition. Not only did he get the audition—he got the job, too. My mother insists that was the start—the launching pad—where Miles first began to be Miles.

The Blue Devils was one of the most popular bands in the St. Louis area. Musicians from all over the country—some from the best bands in the land—would stop by, sit in, and jam with them.

In those days nearly every club that featured live jazz also opened the bandstand to any musician who thought he was good enough to get up there and do battle with the house band or anybody else who happened to be on stage at the time. Jam sessions were the heart and soul of jazz. It was where you learned your craft, tightened up and fine-tuned your game.

My father used to tell me that it was always a "free for all" where it didn't matter what instrument you played. Everybody was challenging everybody else—piano players would be battling horn players and drummers were trying to knock off bass players. It was every man for himself—and the last man left standing was the best.

It was there, in that atmosphere and environment with the Blue Devils, that my father really began to take himself seriously. That's where he gained enough confidence in his playing to keep on playing for real.

Even though he was still in high school, my father managed to work with Eddie Randle for over a year. Miles always acknowledged my mother's role in his joining the Blue Devils, but he still saw the actual start of his career differently.

Sonny Stitt Becomes Impressed

When my father was in a bad mood, he'd say: "Ain't no muthafucka on earth had anything to do with me doin' anything. I just happened to happen." But on most occasions he usually credited Buchanan with getting him to the right places at the right time.

I remember one night he told me that he was doing a weekend gig with some local group—I don't know whether it was the Blue Devils or not—when Buchanan dropped in.

Elwood liked to bring visiting musicians with him to check out his prize pupil. This time it was Sonny Stitt, the only alto saxophonist in those days who even came near Bird—Charlie Parker—in innovation, skill, and style.

The irony of it was that as soon as Sonny saw my father he realized that he had met and heard Miles play with the Blue Devils some time before and that he already had a little history with this kid.

It turned out that after hearing him the first time, Sonny went to my grandparents and tried to talk them into letting Miles go on the road with him and the Tiny Bradshaw band.

At that time Miles was just 16 or 17 and still in high school. So you know that Dr. Davis wasn't hearing any of that playing music on the road kind of stuff. From what I heard, Sonny barely got out of there with his life.

When Stitt heard Miles play, he was impressed with his improvement in such a short time. By now, Stitt had left the Bradshaw band and was playing with an avant-garde jazz band that Billy Eckstine—the former blues singer with Earl "Fatha" Hines—had just put together.

Sonny told Elwood that Eckstine was auditioning trumpet players for what would become his famous bebop orchestra, one which launched the most significant movement in Black classical music.

The story goes that Sonny knew my father had a lot to learn, but he felt that this would be the ideal place for a promising young jazz musician to tighten up his skills. Elwood agreed with him and had Stitt set up an audition. When Buchanan told my father what was happening, Miles couldn't believe it. He thought all hell would break out. But, to his great surprise, it didn't.

Getting Cold Feet

As important as that audition was to him, as bad as he wanted to be in that band, my father got cold feet and started to try and back out of the audition. What could he possibly showcase for Billy Eckstine and his top-class musicians that would make them want him?

What I heard about that incident is that Elwood got really pissed off and did a number on my father's head, asking him, "Why did I do all this for you just for you to put it down?"

I believe it was Elwood who forced my father to get his act together and get ready to audition for that last trumpet spot in one of the greatest bands in the history of jazz. Somehow, Miles managed to make the cut. It seems Eckstine just liked him—saw enough in him to think he could make a real musician out of this kid.

No Traveling with the Billy Eckstine Band

But now my father had a few other problems to deal with. Having cut the mustard with Billy Eckstine caused him some family discord. Miles knew that he would have to go out on the road with the band and do some serious traveling.

The problem here was that although my father had just finished high school, he still hadn't gotten his high school diploma yet. For Dr. Davis and

Mama-Cleo, come hell or high water, without his diploma their son was going nowhere!

There was more trouble. It seems that just before this Eckstine thing, Miles had put his folks through some other changes. In cahoots with Uncle Vernon, he had applied to the Juilliard School in New York City instead of Fisk University in Tennessee, where Mama-Cleo wanted him to go.

Well, when Grandma found out about it she had a fit—and I don't think Dr. Davis was too thrilled about it either. Both of them were very precise and adamant about the direction of his education, although Mama-Cleo and Grandpa weren't always on the same page.

I'm told by people who were around then that Miles and Vernon came on like Clarence Darrow and Johnnie Cochran combined, arguing that although Juilliard's specialty was, indeed, music, it was also rated a highly respected educational facility—a place where my father could study world-class music and get a world-class education at the same time.

My father thought they must have made a pretty good case because that's where he wound up going. Well, with the dust barely settled on that controversy, in stroll Miles and Elwood with news about traveling with the Eckstine band.

My father recalled that he and Buchanan were well prepared to wage this war, showing up with Billy Eckstine himself. He said that Eckstine laid it on thick, saying all the right things—among them, that if he took Miles on the road he would personally guarantee that my father would get three hot meals a day, a cot to sleep on, and, if all went well, a salary too. I also heard that Eckstine made my grandfather laugh by promising him that Miles would wear a condom if things came to that.

I think my grandfather liked Eckstine—his straight talk, strong personality, and rough way about him. I heard that my grandmother kind of liked him, too. But, nevertheless, they resisted. Miles would not get anywhere until he officially graduated.

So the way it turned out, he only got to be with the band for about three weeks. My father said even though he was very disappointed about not being able to work with the band for any real length of time—blowing the chance to go on the road as a member of the greatest band in the world—in those three weeks he grew enormously as a musician and learned musical techniques that he had never experienced before.

The Baby of the Babies

My father once told me it surprised him that nobody in that band was much older than anyone else. Even Eckstine was barely 30. What didn't surprise him was that even at such young ages, all the members of the band were veteran musicians.

Today, the list of band members seems mind boggling. Over the years, players included such all-time jazz greats as Charlie Parker, Sonny Stitt, Dexter Gordon, Gene Ammons, Budd Johnson, Lucky Thompson, Wardell Gray, and Leo Parker on saxophone; Dizzy Gillespie, Fats Navarro, Kenny Dorham, Howard McGhee, Gail Brockman, Hobart Dotson, Al Killian, and, of course, my father on trumpet. Plus people like Art Blakey on drums and the great Sarah Vaughan doing the vocals. Almost everyone in this band went on to become a star in his or her own right.

The youngest band members of all—still teenagers—were Ammons, Leo Parker, the great baritone saxophonist, and my father, who, at barely 18, ran dead last.

I think Miles felt a bit self-conscious. Even these young musicians had been around, playing with top-notch groups. The extent of my father's experience was a stint with Eddie Randle's Blue Devils. To make matters worse, Eckstine (known to most everybody as just "B"), treated all of these young guys as his kids.

He felt somewhat obligated to keep an eye on them. He was the band's unofficial guardian. People who were associated with that band tell me it wasn't long before the three of them became known to the band as "B's babies," with my father having the unwanted distinction of being the "baby of the babies."

Dizzy Gillespie Steers Him the Wrong Way

It was Dizzy Gillespie that he listened to most. (My father once told me that he came up with the nickname "Birks," which was Gillespie's middle name.) And it was Diz, I think, who shaped most of Miles's negative thinking—his intolerance toward musicians who tried to be close to him.

Dizzy was also highly intolerant of musicians whom he felt had extraordinary talent—especially those close to him! He was super hell on young trumpet players. The greater their talent, the harsher his judgment.

Birks believed soul made a great musician—not technique, theory, or style. I remember growing up always being warned by my father that "You can't get no soul without paying some dues. You can't buy it, borrow it, steal it, or imitate it. You got to get your soul the old-fashioned way—you got to earn it."

Treated Like a Slave

My father always believed that the beginning of his adult life, the foundation of what he was about in music, and even his eventual lifestyle took root in those few weeks with that great Billy Eckstine band.

My father often described the members of the band as "renegades." That's what they seemed like to this youngster who had never set foot out of St. Louis. It was a brave—sometimes scary—new world to him, and he desperately wanted to live in that world.

Miles used to like to tell the story about how he and a couple of the young guys once conspired to confront B and other members of the band about treating them like servants.

He said that after he explained their beef, B looked confused and hurt and replied to the effect that he wouldn't stand for that type of behavior from anybody—including himself.

Telling my father that this was an important issue which needed to be resolved immediately, B then called an emergency meeting of the band. He had his "babies" stand up in front of the whole band and told them to get everything off their chests.

The story goes that after the band heard them out, they all went into a huddle. When B finally emerged, he told them that speaking for himself and the whole band, he wanted them to know that they all felt awful about the way the babies had perceived their treatment.

B went on to stress the point that under no circumstances did he or the band members ever mean to treat them as slaves or servants. He said that slavery was something no Black man should ever have to experience again, and that under no circumstances should they ever feel like slaves or servants in his band.

My father used to crack up at this point. He said that following that declaration, B went on to explain that they were in no way servants—they were actually valets, an honorable profession that they should take pride in.

And since they now knew who they were, it would be wise not to bring up that damn subject again. Miles remembered that he and his buddies just stood there looking at B, while the rest of the band sat there laughing.

Boxing and Bar Fights

Billy Eckstine made a strong impression on my father. He was a great singer and musician and everybody in the band respected and liked him. B was a big guy, real tough and extremely good looking. He had a gift of gab and a gift for attracting women. He was always thought of as a man's man.

What I think most impressed my father about him was that he didn't take any crap from anybody—White, Black, or otherwise, band members or civilians. B had some kind of temper. If he thought that he or the band was being disrespected in some way, he'd knock your butt out in a minute.

He was one of those dudes who could cold-cock you with one blow. My father liked B's style—how slick and smooth he was—and how he could be a lot of fun but was not necessarily a fun guy. He liked the way Eckstine handled himself.

Next to music, my father's main interest was boxing. Miles said that somebody was always challenging B about something—his looks, his manhood, his singing, something. He told me that one guy came into the club and told B: "You such a fine muthafucka, you don't need no girl singer in your band, you can be both!"

Miles said that B damn near killed that guy. It took the whole band to get him off that dude. My father liked being in on shit like that. It hurt him when he missed out on that kind of action. He said Birks—or maybe it was Oscar Pettiford—told him about an incident that happened a few months before he got there.

The way I recall it, the band got booked at a joint in Boston where no Blacks had ever worked before. Nevertheless, they drew a pretty good opening night crowd—all White folks, though. But everything was cool; the band played their intros and the crowd appeared to be enjoying the show.

Then B got up to sing, breaking out with "A Cottage for Sale" or some other ballad he used to do. All of a sudden a White woman sitting at one of the front tables yells out at him: "Sing it, Blackie, I love that 'Ol' Man River' voice. Sing your song, chocolate drop."

B got so pissed off by those remarks that he stopped mid-tune, jumped off the stage, went over to the table where the woman was sitting with her escort, and told the guy in a loud voice: "You got the dumbest, ugliest broad in Boston and you got the nerve to bring this piece of shit up here in public. Hide that horsefaced bitch under one of them damn tables in back so don't nobody have to see her ignorant ass."

Well, all the White folks went crazy. It was like a KKK convention or something, and fists flew. B was thumping away at anything colored white. By all odds, the band members should have taken a serious beating, but, as it turned out, they more than held their own.

The audience obviously had no idea that this crew had with them every kind of innovative street weapon available. There were switchblades, brass knuckles, picks, blackjacks—you name it. And the guys who didn't have any weapons on them threw chairs, bottles, and glasses, or just started swinging horns and things.

Whenever my father heard that story of how the band won the battle, it always bugged him. He was disappointed that he missed out on all that good action. Miles was always telling me what he would have done had he been there.

Down and Out in a Boston Jail

My father liked to repeat the rest of the story: Naturally, the cops locked up the whole band, and the charges were too long to count. Needless to say, I don't think too many other Black or similarly complexioned groups ever worked that club again.

And it goes without saying that they didn't get paid, so nobody could make any kind of bail. It looked like the band would be sitting in a Boston jail with no money, no attorney, and no hope of getting out soon.

But along came a Good Samaritan. Somebody not only bailed out the band, but paid their legal fees too. At the time, nobody had any idea who their patron saint was.

Some weeks later, B got a telegram from the guy who footed the bill saying that what happened was a damn shame. He said he had always dug B's singing and admired the work of many of the band members. He wrote that he was glad to help out and wished that he had been there to help kick some ass too.

To everybody's surprise, their benefactor turned out to be Frank Sinatra.

A Friend of Sinatra's

Years later, my father and Frank became pretty good friends. Miles said he once asked Sinatra about that incident—he wanted to know how much of it was true and how much of it was legend.

He said Frank just laughed but never went into it with him. Miles had a lot of respect for Sinatra—particularly his musicianship, breath control, and phrasing. Eckstine and Sinatra were two of the few male vocalists he liked to listen to. When B finally made it big, nobody pulled for him more than Miles—and vice versa. They stayed close friends throughout their lives.

A Change of Direction

In B's band, my father's musical direction, conception, and trumpet style changed drastically. Until then, his major music influences were almost exclusively limited to what he heard local musicians play, swing band recordings, and radio favorites. My father knew all of Harry James's solos.

But from the moment he heard what the guys in B's band were doing, he knew there was another musical reality. He couldn't believe all the stuff these guys were capable of doing. But on the trumpet, it was Birks who mesmerized him with his incredible creativity, dexterity, and facility of execution.

My father tried to imitate everything that he heard Dizzy play. Miles always used to advise young trumpet players to go listen to Birks so that they'd know what to play next.

Junior Mance, the great jazz pianist, said that Miles once told him that any trumpet player, or any musician for that matter, who couldn't learn something from Dizzy Gillespie needed to find another line of work.

Birks, on the other hand, took a liking to Miles's eagerness to learn. I think he got a kick out of trying to teach him what he was doing with his structures, harmonies and techniques. Almost everybody in that band took my father under their wings and tried to teach him something—encouraging his interest and potential.

It was only Charlie Parker—Bird, the real leader of the band—who was less accommodating. It wasn't because he didn't like my father, it was just that he had other things to deal with—among them his drug and alcohol problems.

An Opportunity of a Lifetime

So despite the lightweight teasing and "valet" dues he had to pay, I think my father deep down in his heart felt compensated. He wouldn't have traded that experience for anything in his world at that time.

Miles always considered that part of his life a privilege—an opportunity for tutorship and alliance with some of the people he most admired in his profession. It meant a lot to him to have associated and played with some of the best of the best.

The B thing only lasted a short time for my father. He never did get to go on the road with them at that time. But, nonetheless, his musical, personal, and lifestyle criteria were changed forever.

From that time on, he couldn't imagine a world that didn't include this new type of music and the people he met in the band—particularly Birks and Bird. He had made up his mind that in whatever direction they were going, he would go too.

New York Dreaming

By the time B left town, my father had become a different person. His entire demeanor had changed. He was still shy, introspective, and aloof, but he also appeared to be more upbeat, confident, and eager to test life.

Grandpa and Mama-Cleo assumed his new energy was just the natural excitement any small-town Black boy would have before going to one of the world's great schools in the biggest city in America.

But Uncle Vernon, my mother, and maybe a few of his closest friends knew differently: No doubt about it, Miles still wanted to go to Juilliard. He knew it was the best music school in the country.

But more than that, the greater part of his enthusiasm had to do with being in a big city on his own—a place where Bird, Birks, and all those other great musicians he so admired made their musical Mecca.

Miles knew that some of the guys in the band were going to start smaller groups of their own, and most of that was going to happen in the

Big Apple where music starts and never stops. He just couldn't wait to get to New York City.

What's in a Name?

My father had a private joke he liked to tell about himself from those days. He said for some reason mixed in with all the serious anxieties and concerns he had about his career, it often popped into his mind that there was another contingency that might hold him back from ever being regarded as a truly great jazz musician.

Miles said it seemed like everyone but him in B's band—along with most everybody else he knew in life—all had nicknames; initials, or some descriptive designation of who they were. He said it was obvious that he could never really be anybody when he didn't have that.

"I'm cursed with being now and forever just plain ol' Miles," he would tell me and then laugh. He would jokingly complain that nobody ever thought enough of him to call him out of his name—you know, give him a nickname that fit who they felt he was.

CHAPTER FOUR

Chasin' the Bird
(*Charlie Parker, Savoy, 1947*)

New York, New York

MY FATHER WAS NEVER INTO TALKING MUCH about his early life or life-style—at least with us kids. When he did tell us something about those days it was usually something helter skelter, half-remembered, or half-related; never whole pictures. Mostly stuff with spaces you had to fill in for yourself.

My father was always moody. Me and Squeaky—Little Miles—used to say that he was a man of three main moods: real nice, real mean, and really really mean.

When he was in a talkative mood, whatever he said still had the essence of one-sided debate, temperamental critique, or some kind of controversial diatribe.

But don't get me wrong, he could be a great conversationalist—articulate, well versed in many subjects, and even charming and engaging, when he wanted to be.

Still and all, I always liked to hear my father talk. I used to hang onto every word he would say, trying to picture and remember everything he would tell us about himself. When I was about 12 or 13, I remember him telling us about the first time he came to New York City in 1944.

Barely 18, and being on his own for the first time—especially in New York City—that was big time! From the way he described it, I always thought his first reaction to the Big Apple must have been like Stevie Wonder's from his *InnerVisions* album, when he remarked: "New York! Wow! Just like I pictured it!"

From the very beginning my father loved this big town. This was it. This was always it. But you know how New York is; it always turns out to be much more than you pictured; a hell of a lot more than you can chew. It doesn't play any favorites and you can never take it by storm. I guess my father, like everybody else, learned that the hard way.

Chasin' the Bird

My father wasn't in New York five minutes before he tried to track down Charlie Parker and Dizzy Gillespie, but then so did nearly every other young musician who came to the Apple at that time. Even though both Bird and Birks had told him to make sure he looked them up when he got to town, he found that was easier said than done.

Miles went everywhere people said these two might be—all the places folks said they hung out. He asked everybody he thought might have clues as to how he could contact either one of them, but that did no good.

It seemed like everybody he met knew who they were, and some people had even seen one or the other a day or so ago—that kind of thing—but nobody knew for sure where or how he could find them.

Miles eventually managed to find Birks, who was pretty much a family man. He had a wife and an actual address. Miles always said that Birks's wife, Lorraine, was some kind of a tough customer. She was definitely a no-nonsense sister who didn't cotton much to the traditional jazz musician lifestyle.

The story I heard from my father is that Lorraine kept her husband out of most of the bullshit that a lot of musicians got into—at least when she was on the set. Not that Birks was henpecked or a goody-two-shoes; he was always full of fun, quick-witted, and he loved the babes to death.

They didn't call him Dizzy for nothing. But he generally restricted his wild thing to the road, out of sight, out of town. I don't think Birks ever experimented with hard drugs—certainly not heroin. In other words, he pretty much had his stuff together.

Lorraine liked Miles from day one. He was one of the few musicians on the scene who could come to their house without being cursed and thrown out. It was never just open house at Birks's place.

His wife had to like you, see some character or some socially redeeming grace about you. My father took pride in the fact that Lorraine always invited him in, tried to make him eat and feel at home.

Lorraine took a kind of maternal approach to my father. He was so young, naïve, well mannered, and from out of town. Miles had all the ingredients he needed to win her over.

Very few musicians could make Birks's apartment their headquarters. At one point, Lorraine wouldn't even let Bird into the house. When Parker would come by, she generally made him wait for her husband on the stoop or somewhere outside until Birks would come out to see what he wanted.

She was hip to Bird. She knew he always wanted something from her husband. Sometimes it had to do with music but more often than not he played the same old tune: "Dizzy, dig this!" Then he'd scat out some new concept, chord, or composition in progress, followed by "Hey, you know I love you, baby. Is the Bird still good for a few bucks for a few minutes?"

With Charlie Parker it was always the same old same-old. But the funny thing was, Lorraine really liked Bird and she always recognized what he and her husband were trying to do, and how important they were to the development and execution of the new music. But she just wasn't too thrilled with how Bird mismanaged his career, life, and himself as a person.

Although Birks and Bird were inseparable as a music team—they were the major straws that stirred the modern jazz drink—in their personal lifestyles they were complete opposites. Almost everything Dizzy Gillespie was, Charlie Parker wasn't.

Birks never hung out with Bird on his netherworld excursions. He wasn't a drunkard and/or drug addict, running amok, or self-destructive. So not even Birks had the inside track on Bird's whereabouts.

His best advice to Miles and anyone else who wanted to contact Bird was "Just go down to some good jam sessions, hang tough, and sooner or later, he'll show up."

It seemed that while everybody spellbound by Charlie Parker's extraordinary genius was chasin' the Bird. The Bird, however, was busy chasin' the bag—heroin or some reasonable facsimile.

They say it wasn't that Bird was so mysterious or reclusive, it's just that half the time Bird didn't know where he was himself. And those times when he did, he didn't want anybody else to know. Bird had all kind of folks looking for him, but unlike Miles they didn't all want to kiss him.

Many of them wanted to kick his ass about something—usually money or some kind of drug debt. Then there were many people who didn't care where Bird was, while others hoped that wherever he was he would stay there.

But none of that made any difference to my father. To Miles finding Bird was definitely a major part of his mission. He was determined to find Charlie Parker and nobody was going to discourage him.

Miles Gets Turned Off by Juilliard

In the meantime, Miles was already becoming disenchanted with Juilliard. In fact, he had begun to hate it there. To him, it was dull, super conservative, and inherently racist. He felt it was formatted to theory and composition structured centuries ago by and for well-to-do Europeans.

My father often said he found the school devoid of any contribution by Blacks to the development of any major music. Not to mention the fact you couldn't pat your foot to it.

He began to see Juilliard as just another bigoted institution, promoting the concept of Anglo-Saxon superiority to middle-class Americans in general and to the people called Negroes in particular. He resented the fact that at his chosen place of learning the contributions and achievements of Black people in fine arts were disallowed.

As highly opinionated as my father was, even authoritarian in his attitudes about most things and most people, he was never snobbish about music and culture.

He appreciated nearly all genres of sound and creativity. When it came down to the genuine accomplishments of any people, whatever color, whatever gender, Miles never begrudged them their propers, at least in the context of fine and creative arts.

Bird, Birks, and Miles loved blues, gospel, and classical music alike. They liked to analyze and discuss good music on every front. They always had that in common.

Nowadays, when I think about it, they weren't unusual in that respect. Most of the really great jazz musicians I've come into contact with over the years have had that in common. Coltrane, Monk, Max Roach, Bud Powell, Milt Jackson, Herbie Hancock, Wynton Marsalis: All of them had and have respect for a broad range of musical forms and cultures.

Although I wouldn't dispute my father's assessment of Juilliard at that time—without doubt he had some valid justification—I suspect that along with his objection to its racial criteria, a good deal of his dissatisfaction had to do with the school's curriculum: It didn't include any of the "real stuff" he wanted to learn, nothing that Bird, Birks, and Monk were playing.

The bottom line was they didn't have any courses in bebop. But it really didn't matter what Miles thought about Juilliard, because at that time he didn't have any options. He was there to stay. My father owed that much to Dr. Davis and Mama-Cleo, who had already paid his tuition in full.

He also knew that in order to stay in New York, he seriously needed the money that Grandpa sent him every week. That frustration made him even more desperate to find Bird.

My father once recalled that during the day he'd sleepwalk through his classes, but at night he'd come alive, resuming his Bird-quest, checking out the jazz scene, listening and learning from some of the other great players around town.

Through Birks, who became sort of an escort for him, he was able to meet many of that era's main performers, most of whom he had already admired from records or heard about through the grapevine: Coleman Hawkins, Lester Young, Thelonious Monk, Bud Powell, Eddie "Lockjaw" Davis, Don Byas, Kenny Clarke, Max Roach, Milt Jackson—folks like that. That helped to distract him a little, but he never stopped chasin' the Bird.

Coleman Hawkins Befriends Him

From day one my father would sit in and play with whoever would let him. After a couple of weeks he was jamming in some of the more serious sessions and jazz players began to take note of him, inviting him to play more and even hang out.

Around that time, "Bean," the great Coleman Hawkins, often called the daddy of the tenor saxophone, took a special liking to my father, trying to hip him to what the scene was all about and trying to keep the dogs off of him.

Although Bean fully appreciated Charlie Parker's great musicianship and genius, he wanted Miles adapting to the music without adopting the characteristics of the man behind it.

It meant a lot to Miles that someone of Hawk's stature had befriended him, and most of the time he respected and appreciated Bean's opinions. But when it came to Bird, they couldn't see eye-to-eye. To my father, Bird was the man for all reasons and the man and the music went with the territory.

Getting to Know Freddie Webster

Miles also got really close to Freddie Webster, a great trumpeter, who hardly anybody remembers today. But my father regarded him as one of the "baddest dudes to ever pick up a horn."

He placed Freddie right up there with the best. They got to be like brothers and even lived together for a time. They got to be known all over Harlem and at downtown clubs for always jamming together.

I never got to meet Freddie (who my father called Webs), but Miles talked about him so much it's like I knew him too. About a year or so after they got tight, Freddie died. His death hit Miles hard, but I think it was how Webs died that really got to him.

I never got this part from Miles because he wouldn't talk about it. But according to the grapevine, which can be pretty accurate at times, Freddie and Sonny Stitt, both reputed to be outrageous drug users, were in a Chicago hotel room getting high when Freddie overdosed.

The story that I heard and that went around those days is that when Sonny couldn't revive Freddie, he panicked and left him. At that time my father felt that musicians were supposed to be like brothers and sisters—like family. He thought that Sonny should have stayed with Freddie at any cost. It crushed him to know that Webs went out of here like that—left alone to die.

I don't know how much of this story is true, but whatever happened Miles never quite forgave Sonny for it. It wasn't always an open animosity—he and Sonny still played together, even hung out at times—but my father kept a bad attitude about Sonny after that incident.

The Bird Shows Up

The real high point of my father's first New York City adventure, what he considered the most important and final piece to his erratic bebop odyssey, came when he finally found Charlie Parker. (Miles had briefly met him when Bird was with the Billy Eckstine band and Miles was the new talented kid.)

My father often told me he always remembered the night he finally found Bird or, in a way, I guess you could say that the Bird found him. Miles had gone uptown to jam in some joint and after a few sessions went outside for a breather, just cooling down out front and listening to the music inside.

As my father told it, "All of a sudden there's this voice behind me. 'I see you made it, little muthafucka.'" Even before he turned around, my father said he knew it was Bird! At last, it was Bird!

And there Miles was, just standing there with that half-pained half-smile of his, digging the man he had been looking for so long. Bird broke the spell: "I

hear you been looking for me. What you want, little Nigga? Here I am." They
both started laughing.

Fats Waller used to tell about the time he was working at New York City's
Smalls's Paradise club when Art Tatum walked into the establishment. Fats
was so awed and elated at having Tatum come down to see him, out of respect
he quit playing and told the audience that he was sorry for having stopped for
a minute, but "God just walked in!"

I guess to my father it was that kind of moment. I still remember him saying
it was like all of a sudden everything was going to be all right, because here
comes the sun. He started telling Bird how he had searched high and low for
him since day one—nearly two months.

Miles recalled that Bird just stood there smiling, amused, and not saying a
word. He was just checking him out. Then he walked over to my father, carry-
ing his horn in something like a shopping bag, and hugged him.

My father said he was like a kid, running off at the mouth, trying to tell Bird
where he was staying, how he dug the city, how he had tracked down Birks and
some of the other guys from B's band, about Juilliard—that kind of stuff.

By then, everybody on the scene knew that Charlie Parker was there and a
parade of people began mobbing him like they always did—always in his face,
slapping fives, pulling him into the club.

As Bird moved toward the joint, he grabbed Miles's arm, taking him in too.
Bird introduced him to a few people, sipped out of everybody's drinks, and
then got up on the bandstand.

Miles told me it seemed like Bird was always raggedy, just like he was that
night. He just didn't give a damn about clothes. Even when he was supposed
to be dressed up, you couldn't tell the difference.

My father, who was always into nice clothes, used to crack that Parker wore
Salvation Army clothes, but wherever he got his clothes from they'd almost
always be rough dried and baggy.

The fact of the matter is that Bird thought of most material things as just
objects he could use to pawn or sell when he got uptight, or when he was on a
"rage," which is how he described his drug addiction. He always referred to being broke, raggedy, and half-homeless all the time as his "Spartan way of life."

But Bird was one of those rare people whose presence was so command-
ing that his appearance was never a factor in who he was. And once he put

that horn in his mouth, nobody cared how he was dressed—nobody even noticed.

More Memories about the Bird

My father recalled that when Bird played that night, it was like nobody else was there; everybody in the joint was at full attention, and all the musicians were just standing or sitting there hypnotized—just watching. That's how totally dominating and singular Charlie Parker was.

It was like everybody who knew two hoots about music—musician and civilian alike—understood that however and whatever Bird was going to play next that some new, impossible, and quintessential musical event would be in the making.

As usual, Charlie Parker didn't disappoint anybody. He blew his heart out, creating, crystallizing, opening all those brand-new doors, fine-tuning his contribution to the development of this new movement.

Miles told me that when he heard Bird play that night, he knew and understood for sure why he had come to New York and what he was going to do with the rest of his life. No doubt about it, he had to be a part of this great music.

CHAPTER FIVE

Confirmation
(*Charlie Parker, Dial, 1949*)

The Bird Latches On

AFTER THEY HAD FINALLY GOTTEN TOGETHER, Charlie Parker was seldom out of my father's sight and never out of hearing range. And from what I understand, Bird really liked Miles too. Even back in B's band he felt that Miles was talented and that his interest in music was motivated by more than fame, or money, or as a means to meet women.

Bird was amused by Miles's naiveté, his one-track mindset about music, his eagerness to learn, and, like B, Bird sensed something special about him. Charlie Parker let him hang out with him, took him everywhere, introduced him to lots of bop people, and even let him sit in on his sessions at times.

Miles remembered that he was feeling nearly ten feet tall at all this attention. But everybody who knew Charlie Parker knew he didn't come easy; he always came with dues attached. With Bird you always had to be ready for his ifs, ands, and buts, to win a little and lose a lot.

My father once recalled how Bird just automatically went into partnership with him on damn near everything he had—particularly the little stipend Grandpa always sent.

Whatever else I might say about him, by no means was my father anybody's fool. But in those days, when it came to Bird, he was like Andy Brown with Kingfish on the old 1950s TV show *Amos 'n' Andy*—Andy might've sounded naïve when dealing with the Kingfish, but underneath that façade was lots of cunning.

Becoming Bird's Protégé

Just being around Bird so much, Miles gained a certain degree of acceptance from association. A lot of people just took it for granted that if he was with Bird, he must be a "bad blowing mutha" too.

But my father never wanted something for nothing. He never freeloaded. He busted his behind, learning everything he could from Bird, Birks, Monk, and whoever else had time to teach him. He was a serious and dedicated student of music—that was part of his payback.

Miles often said that as eccentric and off the wall as Bird could be in his own way and without ever trying or wanting to be, he was also a great teacher. He was a stickler for form, facts, and fundamentals.

Bird was always about why and why not, and he never took his music for granted. He never wanted to play the same thing twice, and that's why when playing live he often disappointed his fans; Bird never sounded like he did on his records. With Charlie Parker it was always been there, done that.

Bird liked pushing my father ahead, making him know more than he knew. Miles said that Bird made everything a lesson. If they were walking down the street and a car's brakes screeched, he would say, "What note was that, muthafucka?"

People I've talked to all say the same thing: that Bird loved being this kind of guide to Miles. They say that of all the folks in Bird's circle, the only people who could ever be called his protégés were Miles and Max Roach.

Miles Was a Slave Driver When Teaching Music

My father always denied it, but as he got older certain aspects of Bird's early influence on him would manifest itself. When he was established enough to be teaching other younger musicians, I watched Miles do some of the same stuff the Bird did to him on guys who were in some of his better bands, like Wynton Kelly, Herbie Hancock, Wayne Shorter, Jimmy Cobb, Philly Joe Jones, Tony Williams—musicians like that!

The more Miles loved you, the harder he drove you. The more he saw in you the nastier his tutoring techniques became. It was pure Bird. He was especially hard on Hank Mobley. For some reason, Mobley could really get to him. Miles was always going to "kill" or "whip Hank's ass" about something.

I can't count the times I had to break up some kind of argument between those two. As good as Hank was, Miles always felt he should have
been much better. He complained that "Hank played himself cheap," and
he'd get really mad about it.

I remember that when I started playing trumpet, he was extremely hard
on me too. I still hate to think about those days. I was always on the verge
of tears. I was "every kind of asshole," a "simple muthafucka," a "no-blow-
ing piece of shit."

That was Miles's way of getting me to do better. It was the Mr. Hyde in
him that came out then, although I know that deep inside he really meant
me well.

There were so many times I wished I wasn't his son. I wished I could
just be another musician out there trying to play some horn. I often wondered if I had been just Joe Blow, would his approach to my musical education have been any gentler?

I think it goes without saying that I wasn't too impressed with my father's teaching techniques. Likewise, I'm sure he didn't regard me as much
of a pupil either. But really it went much deeper than that. I don't think he
ever wanted me to be a musician in the first place, like his parents didn't
want him to be.

Starting to Get It Together

As far as peer recognition and public acceptance were concerned, no doubt
about it: Being around Bird had its benefits. Pretty soon most people knew
that my father was the new kid on the block. Then Miles started making a little noise on his own, getting some of his own gigs together here and there.

Miles sensed he was starting to get it together. But he also knew there
was still a lot of space between him and the really good jazz musicians. There
were some terrific trumpet players out there who could show him up.

In those days, a musician who got on the bandstand and wasn't playing
up to par could meet with some frightful consequences from the audience.
Sometimes the heckling and booing got so bad that the entire band would
just walk off the bandstand and leave the horn player up there by himself.

There were times like this when musicians would go over to a horn
player and take his fingers—one by one—off the valves or keys of his horn

and let him know they didn't want to hear any more of his music. Piano players really had to be careful. There were some mean dudes out there who would just slam the piano lid down on their hands.

In some of the uptown places like Minton's, Smalls's, and the Uptown House—joints where you really had to play your heart out—the audience had been known to come onstage, drag a musician off, and bodily throw him into the street. "Don't come back till you learn how to play" was often the refrain that went with the heave-ho.

Miles could always play better than that. But he also wanted his claim to fame to be greater than just good enough not to get dragged off the bandstand. His aim was to crash that upper echelon of truly bad-assed trumpet players that Bird, Monk, and those kinds of geniuses employed in their craft.

Miles wanted to be in the really out-there category of players like Fats Navarro (also called "Fat Girl" because he was so chubby and liked to mock the gestures of what he called "screaming fags"). My father knew that in order to hang tough with these cats, he really had to tighten up.

In the meantime, my father managed to gig some with Eddie "Lockjaw" Davis and Bean, who had their own groups and worked pretty steady. Plus, both of them were musicians who knew what they were doing, knew their music.

So almost according to plan things were falling into place. Miles was moving along and getting better by the minute.

Bird and Birks Split Up

By the time I got old enough to ask any serious questions about those days, Miles was through talking about them. For whatever reason, almost anything pertaining to Bird he preferred to keep to himself.

He was always funny about Charlie Parker. Even though he wouldn't talk about him himself, if anyone else said something snide or negative about Bird, more than a few times I saw him get very Milesish: "Shut the fuck up, you stupid-assed muthafucka. You don't know what the fuck you're talking about, so just shut the fuck up."

He also never made it clear to me exactly why Bird and Birks stopped working together on a regular basis, although I suspect that despite Dizzy

Gillespie's personal love and sense of musical kinship for Bird, it had a lot to do with Parker's unreliability and irresponsible behavior.

In any case, when they split up, Bird was without the brass sound he wanted and needed to give full body to the things to come he saw and heard in his head.

From time to time Bird used Fats, Kenny Dorham, Bernie Harris (the trumpeter whose solo on "How High the Moon" with Bird inspired his groundbreaking bebop composition of "Ornithology"), and a few others.

But as great as those guys were, most of them were junkies, just like Bird, immersed in all the afflictions that junkies suffer from.

So as a band, they never had much of a future. Bird was constantly experimenting with this lineup and that lineup, but when he finally did put a viable group together, it turned out that my father was the missing link.

By now Miles had become much more competent on trumpet. He was reliable and still loved Bird to death. So Bird hired him. This was it! Where he always wanted to be. Playing with Charlie Parker and tapping into all that genius. He was learning the greatest music in the world straight from the horse's mouth.

And it sure didn't hurt that he still had a few bucks coming from home. So money wasn't that much of a priority. At that time, Miles wasn't too worried about whether he got paid. That was good, too, because he usually didn't.

Bird always had a way of liberating the band's earnings under one pretext or another: He'd say that the "White folks" reneged on the bucks or the check hadn't cleared yet, which could be a pretty good excuse because it did often happen that way. But more often than not, Bird just flat out disappeared until he had spent it all.

Becoming the Best . . . and the Worst

Even so, Miles was made for the group. It was then and there that he really began to develop the technique and style that eventually made him even more commercially successful and renowned than his mentor.

Max Roach was usually the power piece of the new ensembles. Sometimes it was Buhaina (Art Blakey), Roy Haynes, Art Taylor, or some other "mean mutha," as my father used to describe them. But for the most part Max Roach was Parker's driving force.

Bird generally rounded out the other part of his rhythm section with as-good-as-it-gets piano players like Bud Powell, Erroll Garner, Hank Jones, Ray Bryant, Walter Bishop, Kenny Drew, Al Haig, and John Lewis.

On bass he liked the real hard-thumping players like Charlie Mingus, Curly Russell, Tommy Potter, Percy Heath, and, of course, Oscar Pettiford and Ray Brown whenever he could get them.

So my father had the best of backup—talented musicians who guided and inspired you to be the best of yourself. That's what Miles always wanted, exactly where he always wanted to be.

It was during this period that my father began to be Miles Davis, the trumpet player. It was also then that he began to be Miles Davis, the Hyde-like something else.

When Miles first came to New York he didn't smoke, drink, do drugs, or hardly ever get involved with any woman besides my mother. At that time, I think most of the young wannabes who came to New York trying to play jazz just jumped into all that kind of stuff like it was going out of style—but at first he didn't.

Maybe they were just trying to be hip. Perhaps they were trying to be accepted by the older dudes. Maybe some of them even thought that lifestyle made them play better. I don't know. But it took my father a while to even smoke cigarettes. The alcohol, drugs, and prowling for women all came a little bit later.

I guess his strict upbringing protected from that self-destructive lifestyle for a while despite the environment he now found himself in. Miles just wanted to be a great musician, to learn and advance his art. As far as he was concerned that's all there was to it. My father didn't want to get into all that other crap.

But it seemed like almost everybody he knew and associated with were junkies, alcoholics, or gamblers, had devastating relationships with all kinds of women, or all of the above.

Most of the older musicians were juiceheads and the younger studs were mainly junkies. All the other vices, they just mixed as needed. In those days, they say, even B fixed at times. It would probably be easier to tell you who didn't do drugs than who did. One thing for sure, the "who didn't" list wouldn't take up much space.

Charlie Parker, who nearly every young jazz player tried to emulate, led the pack. He was almost a *Guinness Book* case study in almost everything that had to do with substance abuse and decadent living.

I was about two or three years old when Miles started doing his drug thing. At that age, nothing about my life changed when Miles became a junkie, but I do know my mother's life changed drastically. My mother was living in East St. Louis at the time and came to New York a little later.

Meanwhile, Bird continued to be prolific and was always in demand. He was always recording. Nearly every jazz record label got him to play something with somebody. He was always jumping from label to label, under contract with one yet nevertheless recording for another—sometimes even using aliases. Bird didn't seem to give a damn about legal things like that. It was just what company paid the most pocket money at the time.

Though my father had cut a few nondescript sides before Bird, his early recording career was almost exclusively with Charlie Parker.

Many people think that many of my father's recordings with Bird's quintets are still among the finest things he ever did. His work with Parker on the Savoy and Dial labels—stuff like "A Night in Tunisia," "Ornithology," "Bird of Paradise," "Don't Blame Me," "Embraceable You," "Out of Nowhere," "Confirmation," "Scrapple from the Apple," "Chasin' the Bird," and "Move"—are among the most important bebop-era recordings and have now become unanimous jazz classics.

From the esteem that came with being Charlie Parker's regular trumpet sidekick, Miles began to get across-the-board recognition from musicians, critics, and the public alike.

During those years with Bird, I don't think Miles ever placed lower than fifth on trumpet in the major jazz polls. It was generally Birks on top, followed by Fats, Kenny Dorham, or Howard McGhee, with Miles fluctuating somewhere in between.

I'm not sure, but I think once or twice my father might have even won or placed second in some polls. So Bird was the best thing that could have happened to Miles regarding his musical aspirations. It was also the worst thing that could have happened to him regarding his character.

I know it wasn't Bird's fault. But in some ways my father went down in flames with him. Bird never wanted Miles to follow him to the lost places. He never encouraged my father to be like him.

In fact I heard Bird was very perturbed and disappointed when my father finally chose terrible dues, the drugs, alcohol, fast babes, and all the related stuff that goes with that lifestyle.

How, why, and for whatever reason he started, it didn't work out well for either Bird or my father. Now that they shared the same music, the same lifestyle, and maybe even the same needle at times, Miles began to think less about where Bird was going and more about where he himself wanted to go.

Although they began to drift apart, in his own way my father still loved and continued to love Charlie Parker as the man for most other reasons. I often wonder who and what my father might have been had he not known and heard the Bird.

Then, again, deep down I know that had he not been exposed to Bird and his lifestyle, there'd probably be no reason to write this book now. Charlie Parker took people to places where they had never been before, places that hadn't even existed before he thought of them.

But kind of like Moses, he also took people to a promised land that wasn't promised to him. Bird took Miles and everybody who walked with or behind him—musicians and fans alike, generations then and now—to a magical music place he was never able to enter himself.

Wishing Charlie Parker Were Still Around

Years later, after my father began to make the big time, every now and then he'd comment more to himself than to us how he wished Bird could have seen and shared his success.

Miles wished Bird could have seen what became of his product, how it had become an important revenue-bearing industry, and a lucrative and marketable Wall Street commodity. He wished Bird, as one of its founders and probably largest stockholder, could share its dividends.

In Charlie Parker's lifetime, I doubt if he ever made more than good plumber's wages. Miles once said that after the industry thieves, taxes, and dope dealers got through with him, Bird used to sit there sometimes, look at the money he had left, look at his horn, and start laughing. Then he'd just go out and get high again.

The irony is that although Bird was often destitute and put himself at the mercy of others, in every other way he was the Man. He was unquestionably the most powerful force and director of his environment. He was treated like a king and the genius he was by the people who knew he was—the lord of the most important new music of our time.

No other person in jazz, with the possible exception of Thelonious Monk and my father, ever approached that stature in the modern music era. As important as Birks, Max, Bud, J.J., Buhaina, and those guys were to the development of bebop, it was Bird who opened most of the doors.

And despite all the problems Miles might have had later on with Charlie Parker on a personal level, he always took a lot of pride in the part he played in helping Bird to open those doors.

CHAPTER SIX

If They Asked Me
I Could Write a Book
(*Columbia, 1949*)

Courting My Mom with Snickers Bars

B ILLIE HOLIDAY'S BOOK, *LADY SINGS THE BLUES*, quoted her as saying that "when my mother and father got married, daddy was 18, mamma was 19, and I was three."

I wanted to open up this book with something slick like that, but in fact when I was born my mother and father were both 20. My mother, Irene Cawthon, was his first love and spouse for many years, bearing him his first three children.

My sister, Cheryl Ann, was his first child. I was the firstborn son and my younger brother, Miles IV, closed us out. I know that probably in the years before my sister and I were conceived—and afterwards—Miles had a few children from other women. I don't know but exactly how many of them there are and I doubt if Miles ever did either. I have met one of them—my brother, Peter Bradley—who has always been supportive of me to say the least.

My father had just turned 16 when he met my mother. At that time he didn't really know anything but music and sports, so he wasn't too swift with the ladies yet. Nevertheless, he flipped out when he first saw her crossing the football field at Lincoln High, where they both went to school in East St. Louis.

I remember him telling me that she was a "bonafide smoker, stacked up, and with a pretty mug." He said, "She had it made in the shade." Plus, he thought my mother had "style."

Miles once told me that my mother was kind of uppity back then, on the sophisticated side and outgoing, while he was the laid-back type and square. When he first spied my mother he was hanging out with two of his buddies, Earl Faulkner and Millard Curtis, both of whom knew her.

My father tried to get them to introduce her to him. Earl told him that she was one of the most popular girls at Lincoln, involved in all the hip school activities, and had a reputation as a talented teen dancer.

What Earl meant is that this was a girl who wouldn't be interested in him. (My father couldn't dance at all. He used to tell people that he didn't dance, but the real deal was that he just plain couldn't dance and never could. It's funny, but most jazz musicians can't dance—including me!).

Earl said that all the slick dudes in school were hitting on her but she always played half-assed hard to get. Miles remembered his friend saying, "Man, Irene ain't giving up shit. She ain't dropping no drawers. She's too slick for you."

To make matters worse, my mother was a few years older than my dad— maybe two or three years. So Earl unkindly added, "Besides, that broad's old enough to be your mamma and she ain't gonna be robbin' no cradle with you."

But Miles was so naïve and corny at that time that he had Earl deliver this message to her: "Miles Davis, my best friend, wants to meet you. He really likes you a lot. And if you go out with him, he'll buy you all the candy you can eat."

That's how slick my father's courting technique was in those days. He thought that candy approach was an offer no sister could refuse. In any case, Earl relayed his message to my mother and, to Earl's surprise, she said okay.

And my dad kept his word. I think he bought her a Snickers bar or something. My mother says that Miles used to think that it was the candy that won him over, but in reality she wasn't the least bit interested in his licorice sticks, Hershey bars—or even the Snickers.

My mom said the real deal was that she had seen him around too, thought he was kind of cute, and wanted to meet him anyway. They were crazy about each other then. Almost inseparable. My mother was his first serious love and it's a fact that she was the first girl he ever made out with sexually.

In any case, what started out with that Snickers bar ended up producing the three of us siblings, none of us more than a year or so apart. We were all here by the time he was 22.

Remembering Miles as a Kid

As a child, what I remember most about my father are random things—specific incidents that just stand out in my mind. Most of the other things I'm telling you about now came from Betty Carter, the great jazz singer, who often acted as a surrogate mother to me, Cheryl Ann, and little Miles.

The rest is from various family members and friends like Clark Terry—people who were around when I was a youngster. The greater and more personal part of my life with Miles really occurred during the time I lived with him as a teenager, young adult, and then in later years.

But if I have one strong impression of him as a child, it's that he had a very dominant personality. The things he said and did, whether we understood them or not, always seemed to have some meaning.

Don't Call Me "Daddy"

My father always had his way of doing things—even back when I was a kid. No doubt, there were times when he wasn't a parent or even a father. There were, however, times when he played all the roles—the caring and concerned father, the provider and protector, the disciplinarian, and the teacher.

But even at our earliest ages, I think all three of us seemed to sense that he transcended just being a parent. It's like we always knew that outside of being our father, he was also Miles Davis, whoever that was.

People often ask me why I always refer to him as my father or Miles Davis, often using both his given and surname. I remember when I was very young I used to hear all the kids call their fathers "daddy" or "papa" or something similar, so it seemed to me that daddy was the appropriate thing to call him too.

But one day, when I addressed Miles as "daddy," he became very cold and stern and told me never to call him that again. He said we should always address him as "father," and only as father, because he was my father—not my daddy.

I didn't quite understood why he got so bent out of shape about that title, but I never thought of him as daddy again. In fact, in later years, I think I just regarded him as Miles, period.

I do, however, have a theory as to why Miles might have rejected the term "daddy." To begin with, Miles was the product of a strong and stable genealogical setting, a family that took pride in maintaining the continuity of its identity, background, and ability to sustain itself by lineage.

Contrarily, too many households that he was familiar with or exposed to were not so fortunate. He had many friends and associates who were the products of single-parent families, whose mothers often had temporary or long-running relationships with a number of male beaux whom they frequently encouraged their kids to address as "daddy" or "uncle."

He didn't like that. He thought there was some kind of stigma attached to the kids who had to go through that song and dance. I think that in his own way Miles was making a statement that he was the actual father of Cheryl Ann, myself, and Squeaky. He wanted it understood who he really was; he was not our "daddy," but our real "father."

Seeing His New Baby for the First Time

When I was born in East St. Louis, Miles was on the road, back in B's band. But he took off for the Christmas holidays to check me out and spend a little time with the family.

According to my mother's account, Miles had burst into the hospital after visiting hours to see me and her. He was very excited about having a son. To him it meant that he had someone to preserve the Davis family name.

During the short time he was back home, so the story goes, he recruited Clark Terry to be my godfather. He told my mother that having Clark in that role made me "official." Clark didn't actually become my "official" godfather until a few years later—but that's another story.

From that time on, I know that my mother, sometimes with me and Cheryl, did a lot of city hopping, back and forth from East St. Louis to New York City to East St. Louis depending on how well my father's career was going, what mood he was in, and, of course, later on which lifestyle he was into at the time.

Whenever I think of East St. Louis, I mostly recall that my mother would be here today and gone tomorrow, depending upon when Miles would send for her and then send her back home.

But Mama-Cleo and Uncle Vernon were always around. They were my major guardians and alternate parental figures during that period. My mother always made it very clear to us—it was just Cheryl and me then—that even though my father was seldom there, we had a father and he was a good one. It was just that his job kept him from being with us for long periods of time.

We knew Miles had to be in New York so that he could make it big and that one day we'd all be together for good, like a real family. That was cool with us, because we were so young and having so much fun. We were busy just loving the ones we were with: Vernon and Mama-Cleo.

He Seemed to Be a Caring Father

One of the things I like to remember about my father in those days was that when he did come home, whether it was in East St. Louis or New York, he seemed to be a caring father.

As soon as he came in, no matter what time of day or night it was, he would come straight to us if we were awake. He'd always play with us for a while—any game we wanted—until my mother came to fetch him. And if we were asleep he'd wake us up, pull us out of bed, and play with us for hours no matter how sleepy we were.

My mother told me that when I was about 18 months old, I swallowed a penny and nearly choked to death. Miles had just come home from somewhere, but during the middle of the night my mother heard me choking and woke my father. He immediately pulled me out of the bed and ran with me to the hospital.

He hardly had any of his clothes on—no shoes or anything—but he got me there in time. I mention that incident specifically because it became an antidote for my anger with him in later years.

Whenever he would really piss me off or we had a serious disagreement about something, I'd try to recollect that incident. I'd recall everything my mother in later years told me about it, and it would soften my irritation a bit.

At those times it made me feel like maybe Miles really did care about me, that maybe he really did have some father in him. After all, didn't he run down the street almost naked to save my life?

Miles Adopts a New Hairstyle

I still remember a period of time in which whenever my father came home he would spend an inordinate amount of time in the bathroom—I mean like hours at a time.

That used to burn my mother up. She was always trying either to get into the bathroom or get him out. But it wasn't about dope then. Would you believe it was a hair thing!?

For some reason he had taken to wearing a "process"—what they called in those days a "conk" or "marcel." That was a hairstyle that almost all the brothers wore at the time. Bird, CT, damn near everybody—even Nat King Cole and B—wore one of those.

In brief, it was a form of Negro hairstyling that chemically lyed, dyed, and crucified your hair into a simulated version of Caucasian hair texture. It took hours to make kinky hair look almost straight, and that's why he spent so much time in the john.

I don't know why Miles was doing it, because his hair was pretty much wavy-straight anyway. It was kind of like Uncle Vernon's with that Indian look about it. But I guess because it was so popular at the time, he must have thought it was hip.

My father wasn't too much up on his politics back then, but hardly anybody else he was running around with was either. In those days, most African-Americans hadn't become "Black Is Beautiful" yet, so they were still accepting the European and White American concept of beauty as a standard for all people.

Looking back, I'm sure none of them had any idea what the straight hair actually represented. Even today, many African-Americans still don't know what it means. They still knowingly or unknowingly try to look like White people.

But that's where my father was back then and, as a child, I thought that anything my father subscribed to was slick. I couldn't wait to grow up and get myself a process too.

Miles's Foul Mouth

While writing this book, my mother and I didn't always agree on what we remembered. Sometimes she would recall something one way and I recalled it differently.

For instance, I remember that Miles used an excessive amount of curse words—muthafucka this, muthafucka that, shit, asshole, bitch, you name it. I think most of the time it was just meant as expression, something to accentuate the positive, although to be sure there were many other times it was meant to be just what it was: something vulgar, something profane.

My mother's memory only recalls a sanitized Davis household where profanity of any kind could not occur, which, on the face of it, was largely true; my grandparents, Uncle Vernon, my mother, and Cheryl Ann almost always spoke in a refined manner.

My father did, too, when he was in that household, but after he left home his vocabulary shrank. By the time I reached talking age, he had pretty much mastered a more vulgar form of speech.

About that time—I was maybe three or four and we were in and out of New York quite a bit then—I got a chance to be around him a little more. Since I was considered his first son, he used to take me to a lot of places with him and introduce me to his friends, and I used to sit there listening to them talk but not understanding anything they were talking about.

I just used to like the way Miles talked. I'd suck up every word he said and the things he did—his expressions and mannerisms. I always tried to copy it all, including his curse words. I think we were living in Brooklyn around the time little Miles was born, and it was then that I really got his speech patterns down.

On one of our returns to East St. Louis, Mama-Cleo was entertaining some of her friends when I walked into the living room and opened up my foul mouth. They were really shocked to hear a little kid like me talking like that.

Grandma apologized to her guests and hauled me into the kitchen at warp speed. I can still hear her scolding voice: "Boy, have you lost your mind?! Where did you learn that kind of language?"

"It's okay, Grandma," I replied. "Father always talks like that."

She tried to explain to me that despite his upbringing and education, my father was not too accomplished in the King's English and that I was never but never to repeat those kinds of words again, no matter who used them.

I remember Mama-Cleo got on the phone and immediately called Miles to discuss the incident. I don't know what she said, but I do know that after she had her little talk with him his language upgraded itself in my presence.

My mother says she doesn't recall that incident. To this very day she still sees Miles as he was in those early years of their relationship—like romantic and all that, at the prom with the corsage he bought her, their walks in Central Park, hunting down movies, and going to stage shows and sporting events together.

She doesn't recall any of Miles's Dr. Hyde side, only mostly the plans, dreams, hopes, and anxiety he had as a young man about his future—all the things they did together before his other darker and more twisted personality took shape. That's the Miles my mother still likes to remember.

CHAPTER SEVEN

Miles in the Sky
(Columbia, 1968)

Learning to Fly High

'M GOING BACK NOW TO A TIME when I was three or four and my father's drug habits had just begun. This was the late '40s and Miles was a young genius still attending Juilliard.

It was during this period that Bird—another genius—had gotten my father on dope, though he never really meant to. For Miles, drugs was a way to fit in—at least that's what my mother told me when I pushed her to talk about a subject she'd rather avoid—and Bird was the delivery man.

My father would say to Bird, "Hey, man, get me a package sometime. Let me try some of that stuff. Maybe it'll add to my blowin'." Miles always got what he asked for.

Miles really didn't have to go that way because he had musicians to hang with like Clark Terry who never touched that stuff. But he was just a young man—about 19 or 20—who wanted to experiment and who was in love with the music of Bird and Birks. So he got too close to Charlie Parker and the Bird's droppings soiled him.

My father split with the Bird sometime around 1950. Miles was a young, talented musician who'd been playing alongside famous and soon-to-be famous performers like the Bird, Birks, Art Blakey, Sonny Rollins, Horace Silver, and Monk. So each day he was getting more and more confident about himself.

It was because he was associated with these "institutions" that he became known as his own man. That's one of the reasons my father wanted to work with these dudes in the first place; he knew that by jamming with them he'd become known pretty fast.

We were living in Jamaica, Queens, at the time—Miles, me, and my mother were all there. My younger sister was at my grandma's in St. Louis, and my younger brother, Little Miles or Squeaky as we called him, hadn't been born yet.

The story that I heard from my family is that Miles used to come home stoned late at night. My mother was a young, square girl from the Midwest and she didn't know what drugs were. But once she caught on, she'd hide my father's shoes so he couldn't go out and cop any bags.

At that time heroin was very strong. You'd get hooked very fast if you were shooting it up. My father had tried snorting the stuff and then somebody told him, "You can get a better rush if you shoot it. It'll be stronger and last longer." So Miles started playing Russian roulette with his life.

That drug thing messed up a lot of saxophone players, although my father was able to come from under it, which I'll tell you more about a little later on.

A lot of sax players died or grew old while they were still young trying to copy Charlie Parker's way of doing drugs. When the Bird died he was in his 30s, but the doctors who opened him up for the autopsy said he looked like a man maybe twice his age.

I don't really remember thinking there was anything strange about my father's behavior back in those days when he was high on smack, probably because I was too young to take any special notice. He had this attitude and that was it.

All I really recall is us living in this apartment, and that we had a kitchen, a bedroom for us kids, and a backyard. His mood swings caused by drugs were not something I paid any attention to. They just seemed a normal part of his personality.

Mostly I remember having fun. I was the only child then until the others came along, so I had lots of attention from my father and mother. That was cool too.

Feeding the Habit

Once Miles was hooked on the heroin it was a horse that always needed to be fed. There's that famous story of how Clark Terry—still one of my best friends—one day found my father laying in the gutter somewhere along Broadway.

CT took him up to his hotel room, cleaned him up, and then Miles cleaned him out—burglarizing most of his stuff. He was really desperate for money. So a couple of weeks after that, Miles got a gig and CT went to the club where Miles was working.

Clark said, "This check is mine," and he confiscated my father's money. They were the best of friends, and what could Miles really say about it after having done what he did?

My father became very petty once he was on dope, and I suspect he was even stealing stuff from the apartment to pawn and support his habit. He didn't mean to, but the urge to get high was more predominant than his principles. Miles needed the heroin and at that time there weren't any methadone treatments. So he did what he had to do. Later on, however, he finally did sweat it out and give up the junk.

The habit also got him into chasing women. Any girlfriend that he was with had to support his appetite for heroin. If she didn't have sufficient means to do so, he'd get pissed off and wouldn't bother with her. Mostly these were beautiful White women who had money and were fascinated enough with my father to buy him what he wanted.

If he wasn't too sick, Miles would also be doing gigs. And that helped him pay for the drugs too. Sometimes when he didn't have a fix he couldn't play or didn't want to play because that would bring him back to some kind of normalcy—and he didn't want any of that when it came to his music.

Drugs turn you into a different being altogether. And from what CT and my mother told me later on in years, that's exactly what happened to Miles. He was not himself anymore—he frequently became a Mr. Hyde. But I didn't see that side of him until many years later.

High on dope, Miles just wasn't the person that his mother and father had raised him to be. My father didn't seem to have any principles or morals anymore. His spirit was some kind of negative force of nature that wasn't entirely a human being any longer.

He Was Just My Father

Like I said, as a child I never saw that side of him. What I do remember is that he was never nasty to me. Miles might've been distant at times or moody, but he never slapped me or anything like that. As a matter of fact, he never once beat me. My mother would do all of that when I deserved it.

I still remember that my father used to come home late at night after a gig—maybe five in the morning—and there were many times that my mother would wake us up for him because he wanted to see us kids. He'd come into our room and say, "Let me see my children." I'd be in night-clothes and I'd rub my eyes and go back to bed.

When I woke up in the morning I'd find these little gifts that he had bought me. There'd be this little plastic horn under my pillow or some toy on my bed. Another thing I remember is how he used to take me and my mother to the old Horn & Hardart's restaurants where you'd put a nickel in these slots and the food would come out.

All I can say is that before he changed for the worst in later years, my father was nice to me as a kid. As an infant, I even took baths with him. Miles was always happy to see his son—he appreciated me—and he had lots of love in his heart for me.

So although these were the beginning of his down-and-out days, I was too young to notice. To me he was just my father. He was Miles and I loved him.

CHAPTER EIGHT

The Man with the Horn

(*Columbia, 1970*)

The Birth of the Cool

THE BIRTH OF THE COOL BAND WAS made up of a talented group, mainly White guys. I think it was around 1949 or 1950, and they were experimenting with a new, easygoing, and orchestrated style of light jazz instead of the hard-thumping jazz sound. That immediately caught my father's attention.

This far-out style of jazz was cerebral, cool, and miles away from the extroversion of the early bebop music my father was used to playing. It was different, and if it was different, Miles was there wanting to try it.

On the piano was John Lewis, Gerry Mulligan on baritone sax, and Gil Evans doing all the arranging. They were a nine-piece band with some other guys whose names I can't remember.

Miles wanted to establish his own sound, and this sounded like it to him. So he took them under his wings. My father was very sought after by the record companies because of his work with Charlie Parker, so he had the clout to put this band on the map and they were more than happy to have him as their sponsor. For them, it was an opportunity of a lifetime.

At the time the record companies were used to dealing with musicians who were drug addicts—people like Billie Holiday. So they knew how to handle creative artists who were eccentric and a little strung out like my father was.

They were more than willing to give Miles what he wanted, and what he wanted most was to do an album with these guys, which he did. However, if what I'm told is correct, the album wasn't greeted with much enthusiasm.

Back then what people wanted was to see some Black man play hard and sweat over his instrument, not just perform some beautiful music. But the Birth of the Cool band had different ideas. They wanted to articulate a certain sound and not duplicate the heavy bebop that was so popular.

So they'd orchestrate music that was closer to nocturnes and sunsets and a beautiful sunny day. It was very original and creative stuff with a very constructed and orchestrated sound—easy-listening music—and it was the genesis of the "cool jazz" movement that caught on a few years later on the West Coast. Even today, you can hear this easy kind of jazz still being played on some popular radio stations.

So What if the Band Was White?

If Miles liked you, he liked you no matter what color you were. He once said to me, "I don't care if a person is green. If he can play like that and he's my friend, that's all that counts." So these White guys from the band got so close they even lived with him at times.

Miles for sure wasn't a racist. Certainly he was very angry at America for the institutionalized racism that this country is hip deep in, but he wasn't a racist at heart.

Anytime you heard Miles say, "You White mutherfucka," it was because he had thought of something this country had done to Black people, not because he hated White people.

My father was stablemates with Gerry Mulligan, Gil Evans, and the other guys from the band, and I remember that Gil Evans always came over to the house. Gil eventually married a Black woman and his son's name is Miles Evans; that's how much he loved my father.

Whenever Gerry Mulligan was doing a gig in Chicago, he used to stay at Miles's sister's house. Miles told her, "Anytime Gerry's in town, let him stay with you."

I remember as a kid how much these guys really loved me, and Miles trusted me with them. They used to babysit for me too. One of the guys from the band once told my father, "Let me take him on a car trip with me and my girlfriend." My father just laughed at that. He thought it was really funny.

Some More Thoughts about Gil Evans

Gil Evans wasn't a young guy when I first met him—at least I don't remember him looking young to me when I was a kid. He was middle-aged.

My father and him were very close, and Gil was the arranger on a couple of albums Miles did—*Porgy and Bess*, *Miles Ahead*, and a few others. They were very close personally and creatively.

They eventually drifted apart because Gil was having personal problems with his first wife, who was an alcoholic, and that was eating up his time. He finally ended up divorcing her and then marrying a Black woman.

I also heard that Gil was always having trouble making money because he was never as famous as Miles. He was having problems getting himself established.

I also heard that later on in years Miles helped to support him, but I don't believe my father could ever give enough back for what Gil did for him musically.

Hearing from the Duke

Besides the Birth of the Cool band, my father was gigging some with other small and experimental groups, trying to keep his hands into everything. He had the time because there wasn't really a lot of work for his new cool band.

Somewhere along the line Miles got a call from Duke Ellington, who wanted him to join his band. But my father had this loyalty to Gil and the other guys, and although he loved Duke and the Duke Ellington band, he didn't want to split on those dudes.

So, as far as I know, he never worked with Duke in a club setting or on any kind of record deal.

The Hotel America

As a kid, I remember that we used to move around a lot. We lived all over New York City, and one of those places was the old Hotel America on 47th Street, before we got an apartment in Queens. For a while we also lived in Harlem, somewhere up around 147th Street, with a Black family named the Bells.

I don't remember too much about the Hotel America, but I do remember that Miles and my mother used to leave me in that hotel room—my sister was still in St. Louis—when they went out at night. They'd come back about five or five-thirty in the morning because they were night people and that's when my father worked to make his living.

My mother still apologizes to me to this day that she left me like that. She thinks that I'm a "bad boy" today, and it's because of those times being left alone in that hotel room without any supervision.

I still remember wondering what time they'd be coming back, looking out the window and waiting on them. I wasn't crying or anything like that, but I was pining for them to come back because I missed them.

I was just hoping they didn't get in any trouble and leave me there by myself. What was I going to do if that happened and nobody came? But, of course, they always came.

People liked me in that hotel and they'd make sure I was okay, so I was never really all alone. I still remember how I used to ride a scooter down the hallways and they'd give me candy and things like that.

Bird Goes Commercial

Charlie Parker got a record deal and they orchestrated him with strings— violin, cello, violas—those kinds of things. I heard some of it and it sounded very beautiful.

Bird got very angry when they took the string section away from him, but the record company decided people just wanted to hear him in a straight-ahead jazz setting.

My father didn't think anything about it one way or another. He certainly didn't think that Bird had sold out like some people had accused him of doing. Later on, when Miles went commercial playing fusion music and wasn't playing what he had played years before, he didn't like people telling him what to do or that he had sold out. He hadn't liked it then and he didn't like it now.

Miles took a dim view of people telling him, "That's not jazz—the Bird's sold out." In his mind, Bird was a genius and he could do anything he wanted. Birks and Bird were his idols, and they could do nothing wrong.

Bird's Death

Charlie Parker died in March of 1955. I remember how sad my fatheer sounded whenever I heard him speaking about it. He would just shake his head and get into a different mood altogether.

He'd never voluntarily talk about Bird's death, but sometimes someone would come over to the apartment and bring the subject up. It'd make him so sad that he'd have to leave the room.

Miles had come all the way to New York to find Charlie Parker, and now the one person he really idolized was gone. My father loved the man and appreciated him as a genius. But the Bird was no longer flying, and I think that left an empty spot in my father's heart until the day he died.

CHAPTER NINE

Milestones
(Columbia, 1958)

Going Cold Turkey

I THINK IT WAS SOMETIME AROUND 1955 that my father just about had it with heroin. It was using him up and he had bigger things planned for himself than being a strung-out junkie.

Me, my father and mother, and my little brother Squeaky were all living in the Bedford-Stuyvesant section of Brooklyn.

Miles decided that the best place for him to sweat it out was Mary Francis Manor, his father's farm in St. Louis that was named after Dr. Davis's mother, my great-grandmother.

It was there that Miles quit cold turkey, locking himself in a room until he stopped his cravings. One version of the story goes that my grandfather chained him to a heating pipe until Miles could sweat it out. All I know for certain is that it was a very trying time for my father.

I was about 11 or 12 years old then, and my mother never told me about Miles sweating out any dope or anything else about his addiction. I learned all about it in later years and what he had done to clean himself out.

Miles just left us and there was no explanation from my mother. The only thing she said was that he'd be gone for a while. I'm sure he got some urging from my grandfather to come back home and clean up his act.

The story I heard was that Miles was playing out in California and he had to run all over the place to get drugs because connections weren't so familiar or reliable over there. It wasn't like New York City where bags were easily available all the time.

So my father decided it just wasn't worth it—it was just too much of a headache and he was tearing himself apart. Not only was it a pain in the ass to get hold of the dope, but it was poisoning his system too. He just made up his mind to quit.

I think he was realizing that he was going to make a lot of money with his talent, and that record companies weren't going to accept him being a heroin addict even though they'd put up with some other strung-out musicians like the Bird and Billie Holiday. Miles felt he was just getting too strung out even for himself.

Back then my father already sensed that he had the potential of becoming a big star if only he'd leave the heroin alone and stick to his business. So he went cold turkey. On my grandfather's farm there was a huge five-bedroom house, always fresh milk, and a maid who'd cook whatever Miles asked for.

It was a wholesome change of pace that my father much needed. On the Fourth of July, my grandfather would even invite the Boy Scouts to his farm and they'd camp out, go fishing; sometimes Miles would do a little fishing himself. He had everything he needed there except the medicines that a hospital could provide.

Thinking back about how my father came out from under his addiction, I'm really impressed by the willpower it took on his part to do it. So I'm really proud of him for weaning himself off that junk.

I'd say he was away from us six months to a year. All that time he was getting himself physically in shape to play the horn again and to think normally about doing something other than going out there to buy drugs.

You see, dope addicts make it a lifestyle. Thinking about your next fix becomes part of your everyday reality. Miles had to get rid of those ideas and fantasies and put blinders on like a horse at the racetrack and stick to thinking about his life and his career and his music.

Living by Himself

When my father finally did come back to the city, he was no longer interested in living with my mother way out in Brooklyn. He got himself an apartment on 57th Street and Tenth Avenue.

Diahann Carroll and her family had an apartment on the same floor in the same building, and I don't know if she arranged for Miles to get his place. I guess the reason my father decided to live on his own was that he got too big for his own self. Although my mother was intelligent, she was just a good country girl that had his children, and he figured he could get any other girl he wanted.

He had met other women with certain independent means and this and that, so he grew out of my mother; they grew apart. Miles was becoming famous and my mother didn't have what he wanted or needed anymore.

Whenever I visited him—which was pretty regularly—Miles would always send me back with 25 to a hundred dollars to give to my mother. In 1955 and 1956, 25 dollars was a tidy sum. A loaf of bread back then only cost a quarter.

I don't know much more about what went on between the two of them, but I do know that my father was now making a new beginning in more ways than one. He was all cleaned up and no more chasing Bird or the bag. He was full of energy and eager to jump-start his career.

My father resumed his collaboration with Gil Evans, and they started rehearsing together. That collaboration would last into the 1960s, as they turned out big band albums like *Miles Ahead* and *Porgy and Bess*. The last one they did together was *Quiet Nights*.

Weekends with My Father

I was 11 or 12 years old and I'd usually spend weekends with my father in his new place. I remember that it was a big studio apartment with a large living room, a kitchen, and a bathroom. Miles had a grand piano there and his bed was in one corner of the room.

My brother and sister would sometimes come with me, but I was the only one who stayed over on weekends. I used to sleep on the floor on a small pad. I guess my mother made these arrangements with Miles that I would come over and get the money because she needed it to support us.

She was working at the time as a secretary or a receptionist at Brooklyn Jewish Hospital, but the pay wasn't much. My mother had beautiful handwriting, she could type, and she had secretarial skills. One thing I'll tell you, no matter how tough times sometimes got, we never saw a day of welfare or ever received any public assistance.

My father always liked cars, and parked outside the apartment was a 190 SL Mercedes. After the 190 SL he began to buy Ferraris. An expensive apartment on his own, fancy cars—Miles was becoming successful and making money. He had put those blinders on and was focusing on his career—not dope—and it was starting to pay off for him.

Usually when I came over my father was hard at work. He'd be busy writing and composing; I remember there'd always be sheet music all over his piano.

Sometimes Bill Evans, who was a great piano player, and Gil Evans were there with him, working out changes with my father for some new song. Other times Wynton Kelly, another great piano player, would drop by.

I'd be looking at TV and they'd be over in a corner, constructing their music. When I wasn't focused on the television or playing with something, I'd watch them and listen to them make music. I understood this was my father's work—that he made albums—and that they were trying to create music. These fellow musicians would come over and get on the piano we had. They'd be talking about voicing a chord or arranging a melody—but I wasn't much interested in all that.

When my father wasn't busy, we had great fun doing all kinds of things together. We ate chicken out of a box, and I remember once that he took me to the store and bought me a catcher's mitt. Then we'd go to the park and play some ball.

During this time my family was living in Bed-Stuy, a really tough Black neighborhood out in Brooklyn. I was kind of an easygoing kid, and the other kids in the neighborhood used to pick on me. So one day my mother told Miles, "Hey, you better take him to the gym or something. You need to teach him how to fight."

My father loved boxing. It was his favorite sport. Miles knew this guy, Johnny Grinage, who had a community gym going.

One day Miles bought me some boxing gloves, and he took me over to the gym. He said to Johnny, "Take my son and teach him how to fight. Give him some pointers in boxing."

He gave Johnny some money and from that day on I had a personal trainer who taught me how to box. After that, I used to beat up everybody who picked on me. They never picked on me anymore.

I remember once asking my mother why people have to fight, because I wasn't that kind of a person. All she said was, "We're living in Bedford-Stuyvesant. You'd better learn something."

There were other really nice things I remember about those weekends I used to spend with my father, like how we'd just jump in a cab and go to Yankee Stadium to see the ballgames.

He'd also take me to Madison Square Garden to see the fights. Then there was one Christmas when my father bought me and my sister Raleigh bicycles, and I remember how the smiles on our faces made him so happy.

Sometimes we'd do nothing and Miles would relax by listening to the radio. His favorite station was the classical one, and his top choice of music was cultural European music. He'd listen to Stravinsky's *Rite of Spring*, Bartók, and Rachmaninoff, and me along with him. It was my own exposure to all kinds of music.

If it wasn't classical, then he'd be listening to Ray Charles, James Brown, and lots of funk. Anything that was inspirational to him my father would be listening to it.

I had been playing drums and a little trumpet since the time we lived in St. Louis, and my father would keep me practicing. He'd drop little lessons on me, playing his horn and having me copy what he was doing. Believe me, it wasn't an easy thing to do.

He wasn't the kind of guy to sit down and give you a whole outline of this and that. You'd have to take it as he gave it to you and when he felt like it. Miles would say, "This is how you play a high note, Gregory. Listen."

And I'd try to do that. If I made a mistake my father would say, "I don't want to hear that anymore. This is how it's done." Then he'd play the note again.

When he wasn't working at his apartment or hanging out with me, Miles was doing those big band recordings with Gil Evans. He also had a small quintet that he played with. Since drying out, he was chock full of energy.

This whole time my mother never once mentioned anything to me about how Miles had battled to get over his heroin habit. I learned all about that later on.

She must've been pretty even-tempered about the situation because I hardly remember her ever getting angry at him. There was one time, though, that I do recall her blowing her top at Miles.

My father was supposed to do something that he evidently didn't do to her satisfaction. She called him a "Jive-ass muthafucka—a JAM." She said to me, "When you go see your father, tell him he's a JAM—a jive-ass muthafucka."

I laughed, went to see my father, and repeated the message. After being angry for just a minute, he almost fell down laughing.

Miles Gets Really Pissed

Around that time my father had a sextet that included John Coltrane on tenor sax, the ex-fighter Red Garland on piano, Paul Chambers, and Wynton Kelly. Later on there was Bill Evans and Cannonball Adderley. Cannonball was a great musician, and so was his brother, Nat, who played cornet, with Cannonball on the alto.

I must have been about 12 years old when out of the blue Miles said to me, "Come on, I'm gonna take you gigging in Chicago." My father wanted me around because I think he really wanted me to know him and understand his lifestyle and also to get me away from the women in the family.

I remember that we flew to Chicago in a propeller plane because they didn't have jets yet. When I got off that plane I was feeling like I was seasick or carsick. I think he was a little late for the gig, so we jumped in a cab and we went to this club called the Crown Propeller Lounge. I was so sick to my stomach that I was turning green. When we got there, I had to go to the bathroom and puke.

I came out and Miles was already onstage. He said, "What song do you want to hear, Gregory?" And I said, "'Dear Old Stockholm.'" I liked that song because of the beat.

As I said, I used to mess around with the drums when I was that age, so even though I was still feeling sick he called me up and he had me do my little drum solo. He said, "Gregory, come up here and play a little drums." So there I was, onstage behind him and Philly Joe Jones. I was so excited I forgot about being sick. It was little kid stuff but I sure remember it.

Being a shy kid, I was really wide-eyed and shocked that he would ask me to come up onstage and play anything. But I guess he was proud of me and he wanted the audience to know that he had a kid who could play drums.

Another time we showed up at some club in Chicago, again, and this promoter had Miles going onstage third. He had, maybe, five different acts—singers, different bands, stuff like that.

My father didn't like it at all. He wanted to go on first, and he did! So when it came time for the promoter to pay him off, the guy says to him,

"Miles, I'm docking you five hundred because I told you that you don't go on first."

Well, that was too much for Miles. I was standing there and I saw him get real mad. He just reached over this desk and pulled this dude out of his chair. Before I knew it, Miles had him on the floor and was whupping his ass.

Cannonball Adderley must have somehow sensed something was wrong because he came running in and pulled my father off the guy. Cannonball was a big guy, and that's where he got his name from. He said to Miles, "Whatta you doin'?" Miles wanted to continue to kick that guy's ass, but Cannonball broke it up. I think the promoter ended up suing him.

That was the first time I'd ever see my father go off like that, and I was wondering what the real reason was other than the money. Then, later on in life, because I played the horn myself, I understood.

I realized how very hard it is to play a trumpet with all the sweat and blood and energy you have to put into the instrument, and then for somebody to try and shortchange you. It would make you very unhappy, and Miles was uncontrollable at that moment.

Except for that night at the club, I don't recall my father at that time in my life ever showing his Mr. Hyde self— or, if he did, I still was too young to notice it. I just knew that he was a good father to me and he did the best he could.

My father was still keeping himself busy, and by 1959 he started using modes or scales instead of chord structures. That experiment resulted in his famous *Kind of Blue* album.

I don't want to get into a whole technical thing, but basically he was using modes and tones that folk and cultural composers like Gershwin and Stravinsky used. He loved the Dorian mode and that record was built off that.

Coltrane Steals the Spotlight?

A lot of stuff was written about Miles saying that during this period Coltrane stole the spotlight from him as the innovative style setter. That's just not true. He never stole the spotlight from Miles Davis when he was in my father's band.

Coltrane happened to be an exceptional musician and he was beginning to be recognized. He'd played with Monk and, later, worked with great players like Sonny Rollins.

He was different in his approach to music because he had so many ideas that were very spontaneous and original when he was playing his horn. That's why my father hired him in the first place.

Sometimes Miles would say, "I pay this muthafucka so much money to sound like he's practicin'." Coltrane was all over the place. People thought it was interesting and they were trying to figure it out. Some people didn't like it at all.

It wasn't that Coltrane stole the spotlight from my father, it was just that the music he was playing was very controversial because he was not playing it the standard way, and that got people talking.

My father and Coltrane did eventually split, but not for any special reason. Miles always changed people who were in his band. Coltrane left Miles the final time because he got a record deal, not because there was any animosity between him and my father.

He had become established and wanted to be out there on his own. Over the years he had worked with Thelonious Monk and a lot of great people, and his last stop before doing his own thing was with my father's band. But now he had his own record contract. His sound had become recognized.

I once met Coltrane as a kid, and he was a great guy who loved my father. I remember one time, when he was sick with the liver cancer that would kill him, that he came to the brownstone Miles owned at 312 West 77th Street. My father had been able to buy the building after winning a lawsuit that involved a cop beating him up outside Birdland.

Miles had a gym in the basement and he told me to go down there and demonstrate punching the bag to Coltrane. I was always demonstrating punching the bag to somebody. Miles would always be saying, "Yeah, go down and watch my son hit this bag." He'd say to me, "Hey, Gregory, go down there and hit that bag for Coltrane."

It always annoyed me at first when he did that. I would be doing something like my homework or watching TV and he would interrupt me. But after I got down there and did it I realized it was for everybody's enjoyment, so I didn't really mind so much. My father would expect you to jump up if he needed you regardless of what you were doing. He'd do this to me most every time someone dropped by the house, like the great pianist Wynton Kelly and Paul Chambers, who was a great bassist.

So Coltrane came downstairs and I guess it made him feel a little better seeing me do this, because he was in such bad health. He probably was thinking, at least there's a young man comin' up who's got his body together.

My father and I thought that Coltrane was a great guy. We were both very sad when this great musician died.

A New Quintet

Throughout the '50s Miles led bands that featured greats like Red Garland, Bill Evans, John Coltrane, and Cannonball Adderley, and in the early '60s he put together a new quintet with Herbie Hancock on piano and Wayne Shorter, who was a great composer and also played the tenor sax. It was a very special group because they were exploring sound, and Miles always liked that energy from younger players.

The older players always wanted him to stay in that familiar jazz mode, but my father's genius was too restless for that. He was always looking for new directions in musical form. So he'd pick young musicians to play with who were thinking along similar lines.

A lot of times when they were playing they'd go outside the song, so to speak, because of all their energy, and it was a great phenomenon to hear. The music sounded good and everybody would say, "Wow!"

But it was always my father who controlled the locus of sounds, which was spectacular in itself. They'd all draw this energy from the music and from each other.

From Fusion to Hip-Hop

I know I'm jumping way ahead, but it fits in with what I've been saying about my father always looking for new directions in his music. He was, as they say, miles ahead.

Sometime around the early '70s my father was forging full steam ahead into an experimental sound known as "fusion." He was getting tired of playing bebop because, as usual, Miles felt it had gotten stale and was boring to him.

Once more he was looking for new directions, and it was then that with his horn he announced the arrival of a musical form that critics termed "fusion," which is why he was into rap music and hip-hop before hardly any White person ever heard of the words.

Even in the 1990s, just before my father died, he was searching for something new and different. That's when he first started listening to hip-hop. Miles didn't think it was something that was going to revolutionize music. It was just a sound that he knew was starting to emerge, and he thought he'd better get aboard the boat or be left behind.

My father didn't do any concerts with hip-hop musicians, but he appreciated the certain thing that they had, and he took that sound just like he did with rap and used some of it in his music. Miles would always take what he could incorporate into his sound and leave the rest behind.

Very few artists I know to this day are able to do that—to look around at other artists and then incorporate what they hear into what they do without sounding like someone else. My father took some things from hip-hop, from rap, from classical music like Stockhausen and Rachmaninoff, and even from Gershwin, and then blended it into his own style.

Miles never turned away from the so-called "cool jazz" or bebop as some accounts of his life state. He was always a "cool" player—that was simply his style. He just speeded it up a little and got a different beat to make this new music. He didn't try to play all over the melody and embellish it the way some guys did.

Why would an artist trash something that had been useful to him? My father simply incorporated bebop into his new style of playing, which was always there in his sound.

If he had a melody, he'd play it straight and cold and leave it as it is. He'd let the piano or whatever other instrument take it out, then he'd come back in and play the melody. Miles never got away from his theory of leaving space for the sound and he never got in the way of the melody.

Heroin Didn't Beat Him

Getting back to my father's "down and out days" as a heroin addict, all I can say is that in my presence he never acted like a junkie—just sometimes moody, but otherwise appearing normal.

Reflecting on it all, I'd say it was Miles's willpower and my grandfather's insistence that my father got his act together and became strong again. My grandfather just wouldn't let a Davis—especially his own son—be like that.

He was a powerful man and would rather chain Miles up to a pipe and see him die before he'd let him come back out and be a junkie. It was the Davis family legacy. They were always accountants, lawyers, dentists—professional people—never dope addicts.

Getting into drugs was not something Miles fell into because of his family background, but because of some people around him. So he had to get away from that crowd and come out of that house clean if he was going to accomplish anything with his life. He also had to face his father's judgment and maybe that was the biggest impetus of all for him to clean up his act.

Miles was able to come out of that heroin addiction with a lot of power and creativity as far as his music was concerned. I think it's because he put all the energy into his music that he would've otherwise invested into the pursuit of drugs.

I was in junior high school at the time my father was sweating it out and still living with my mother and my siblings in Brooklyn. But then in 1958 or 1959 when my father bought a five-story townhouse at 312 West 77th Street in Manhattan, I moved in to be with him along with my siblings, Cheryl and Miles IV.

It was a good time for my father when he got back and was busy performing in concerts all over the world with the likes of Sonny Rollins, Horace Silver, and Monk.

Cocaine Running through His Brain

But drugs would once again get hold of my father. It was the 1970s and his drug of choice this time around was cocaine—he would never again touch heroin. Even the thought of it would make him sick.

I remember years later, when he felt comfortable enough to talk to me about his heroin addiction, Miles would say: "I'll never go back to that." Once he told me that when he was sweating it out, he smelled like "chicken soup."

With the heroin, it was peer pressure that rubbed off on him and got him into it in the first place. You have to be strong enough to say "no," but he just wasn't.

He knew heroin was not something to be messed with, yet nonetheless he embarked on that dangerous journey especially since his role model, the Bird, was also traveling along that perilous route.

Yet he was able to come from underneath it and go on to become a great musician. He lived his dream and was able to put out all this great music. Miles was a fighter and never let heroin beat him, and I still admire him for that. The cocaine, however, was something else.

My father established a new fusion band sometime around 1969. It was Jack DeJohnette on drums, Dave Holland on bass, Chick Corea on piano, and Wayne Shorter on tenor sax. That's when he also established his new drug habit.

Miles had beaten the heroin but now he was feeling empty. It was his personality that made him start messing with this stimulant. He wanted to be with different music, different women, and different drugs; my father was always an experimenter.

Back when he was doing heroin, he thought that because Bird and other musicians he respected used it that it enhanced their playing and would do the same for him. So he tried it.

But I don't think that with cocaine it was like that. Miles wasn't using it to enhance his music, but more for recreational reasons. He now had the money to buy it, and he also knew that it would draw women—especially younger women—and that gave him pleasure. My father also had the time to get into coke because he had taken one of his many "retirements" from music.

He'd been playing with his new fusion band, and felt that Chick Corea was really something else. My father thought the group really took the music outside, and that Corea played somewhere else in the stratosphere—to a different dimension, which is where my father always wanted to be.

This band was the one Miles had right after Herbie Hancock and Tony Williams, and for a while he was really digging it. But after a while, Miles grew restless again.

My father didn't know what to do next to keep growing and exploring musically. He felt like he had already played everything, and so what new and creative ideas could he bring to music?

In addition, people expected so much out of him that he didn't know what he should be playing to meet that expectation—especially because he was someone who was always looking for new directions with his music and he knew that his fans expected that from him.

So Miles decided to lay off from performing. He just wasn't hearing or doing anything new musically. My father took a "sabbatical," and with nothing to do he became like a fish out of water for three years. He'd just stay at home and use more and more cocaine.

He was kind of like a fighter or an athlete. Onstage when he was performing, his energy was high and that was an exhilarating feeling. But at home, when he wasn't working and just doing mundane everyday things, he missed that feeling. Coke helped to lift him up and go a couple more rounds.

My father, at this point, was like a racehorse with blinders on. A racehorse wants to run all the time, but the blinders stop him. Miles was kind of like that. He wanted to run fast all the time, but he wasn't always onstage so he didn't know what to do when he was just sitting around.

My father used to go to the gym to work his energy out, but after he had his hip operation he couldn't do that. So he resorted more and more to cocaine. It gave him an exhilarated feeling like he was onstage.

CHAPTER TEN

Quiet Nights
(*Columbia, 1962*)

Messing Up His Voice

I WAS AROUND 1957, and I was 12 years old. Me, my mother, my sister, and Squeaky, who was just a baby at the time, had just moved out of our apartment at 33 Troy Avenue in Brooklyn and we were now living in Chicago.

I don't know exactly the reason why we moved, but we relocated to the same apartment building where Miles's mother lived. I was just getting ready to enter Carter Elementary School on South Michigan Avenue. Miles, meanwhile, was still holed up in his 57th Street digs.

This was the time when my father's voice would never sound the same again. Miles had gone to the hospital to remove a couple of nodules from his vocal cords. The doctor had told him no talking for a while—especially no yelling.

But just two days later he got angry at this promoter and started yelling at him on the phone. The end of the story is that Miles messed up his voice for the rest of his life and got that trademark hoarse sound when he spoke.

When my father called and talked to me on the phone, at first I thought maybe he caught cold and it would go away. But it never did. He was stuck with it. I don't think he ever liked the way he sounded, but it wasn't something we ever discussed.

Reuniting with Coltrane

My father hired Coltrane back to become part of his band sometime around 1958 because people wanted to hear more of him. "Trane was the only one who knew all the tunes," my father jokingly said about the return of his old friend.

There was never a bitter thing going on between them, and so Coltrane appeared on *Milestones* and *Kind of Blue* along with Cannonball.

This stint with Miles made Coltrane even more popular, and Coltrane ended up with a new contract from Atlantic Records—partly due to his playing with an institution like my father was, and no less because of his own special genius.

Miles at His Funkiest

Around 1969 or 1970 my father started listening to a lot of Sly Stone and James Brown. Later on, he was also listening to a lot of Prince. As usual, my father was trying to get some fresh musical ideas to incorporate into his own sound—trying to get his music a little more bluesy and funky.

He just wanted to move away from the jazz paradigm of doing things. Miles was a consummate musician, so he was able to absorb and get something out of all kinds of music—classical, rock, folk, you name it.

The album *So What!* is even built up around some James Brown melodies. If you listen carefully, you'll see that it has a mixed jazz, soul, and funk sound to it.

Some accounts of my father's life during those years claim that he was losing touch with his core audience—especially in 1968 when Miles began experimenting with rock and electronic music. But, again, that's just not true.

Miles was just losing touch with those people who wanted him to stay in one musical idiom all the time, playing basic jazz over and over again. My father had made his reputation by being different. He went from the Bird to the Birth of the Cool, and people appreciated him for making those changes and being so innovative.

My father was always known for looking for new directions in music, and he wasn't going to stop now. He once said in an interview that those "little phrases" he used to play in bebop wouldn't fit today's music, and today—make it tomorrow—is where he wanted to be.

Miles always wanted to be in the vanguard of music, not a follower of some style. He liked to use the word "avant-garde" a lot. My father was an artist who always wanted to lead the way.

Sure he could play that bebop and cool jazz, and he could play it well. But Miles thought it was time for him to change—after all, that's what his audience was always looking to him to do.

I remember that even during that little hiatus when he dropped out of performing altogether, musicians were always coming by the house and saying to him; "Whatta we gonna do, Miles? Whatta we gonna play? Why don't you come back out?" They were looking to him for direction too.

And my father would start laughing. He'd say, "I don't know. I don't know yet. When I know I'll let you know." What he was trying to put together now was a mixture of soul, funk, and jazz in his own creative way. And rock and electronic music was part of the equation he was trying to create.

Some of these articles about him claimed not only that he was losing touch with his core audience, that he was now more interested in playing White clubs and expensive neighborhoods. That's bullshit too.

Miles always played at clubs where all kinds of people appreciated his music—rich, poor, White, Black, English-speaking, and non-English-speaking. He was not out to play before an exclusively White audience.

I mean, he was a top artist and had a contract with one of the top record companies, so he'd always do concerts before a mixture of races—although sometimes most of the people sitting there were White because they were usually wealthier than Black folk and could afford the high ticket price.

Learning a Lesson from Jimi Hendrix

My father was always trying to reach a young audience. Classic jazz was becoming like a relic, a collector's item to him. It was the older people who wanted to hear those Miles albums with Charlie Parker, but not the young— especially the young African-Americans he always wanted to reach.

Miles really dug Jimi Hendrix. Miles was introduced to Jimi around 1968 by Betty Mabry, who later became Betty Davis. There's the old rumor that Betty was unfaithful to Miles and slept with Hendrix. Whether that's true or not, Miles had a lot of respect for Hendrix. The two became friends. I remember that Jimi was performing at the Isle of Wight Festival. It was just before Jimi died in 1970. Miles was playing at some club. So Betty set them up, and he and Hendrix got to small-talking. "Yeah,

I'm working another festival," Jimi told Miles. "I'm playing maybe before a hundred thousand people."

"Say what?" my father replied. "And I'm workin' in this little joint?" Hendrix was performing before thousands, and my father was playing before much much smaller audiences. You have to remember that rock was always more popular than jazz. Rock stars were known for large venues, but back then jazz greats like my father played mostly clubs. Jazz was always more esoteric, while rock had wide popular appeal.

But this conversation clicked something in my father's brain. It started him thinking. "Yeah, I think I should be really concentrating on large venues," he told Hendrix. He knew that these rock stars were making big money when they played at places like Madison Square Garden and New Jersey's Meadowlands Arena.

Miles knew he was an established star and that his name was big enough. Why shouldn't he get paid as much as these rock stars? So that's what he started to do, even appearing at the Isle of Wight Festival with Hendrix, Jethro Tull, the Who, Ten Years After, and others. There was also the Amnesty International Concert that Bill Graham produced in 1986 at the Meadowlands Arena. The concert, which drew a fantastic 138,000 people, featured Miles, U2, Peter Gabriel, Fela Kuti, Richard Pryor, and many others. It was a huge media event.

My father became one of the first jazz musicians to make this changeover to really large venues. He didn't even have to be on a bill with other people—he could draw crowds playing all by himself on the stage.

This was one of the lessons he learned from Hendrix. Now Miles started playing at really large concerts all over the world and got out of that stagnated routine of jumping from one gig to another at some club.

Sure he still did clubs, but the money had to be really right and it had to be a large capacity crowd. If the club couldn't hold enough people, he wouldn't be there.

He Didn't Even Go to His Folks' Funerals

Hendrix and Miles traded ideas and discussed projects that, regrettably, never materialized. He adored Hendrix, so when Hendrix died Miles went to his funeral out of respect. It was the only funeral my father had ever gone to.

He didn't even go to his mother or father's funerals. They died sometime in the early '60s. My grandfather went first, and then my grandmother. It wasn't that he didn't love his parents, it was just that he couldn't stand being there burying them even though he paid for both their funerals.

Miles was too sensitive for these kinds of things. He didn't want to see them like that, so he stayed away. Some people have a fragile state of mind when it comes to confronting death, and my father's tolerance was very, very low. According to those who witnessed Miles sign his own will, he never even read it. Attending funerals, reading his own will, it would've affected him too emotionally and physically, and he just couldn't handle it.

Meeting Prince

James Brown, Hendrix, Sly Stone, Michael Jackson, and Prince were all performers that Miles admired. Since he was a big fan of James Brown, Sly, and Hendrix, it's no surprise that when he heard Prince's music he connected with Prince's sound. Miles even did some work with him on an ill-fated two-CD set. One disc was supposed to be a hip-hop album, and the other reworkings of sessions originally for a Miles project called *Rubber Band*, with tracks contributed by Prince.

They appreciated each other's artistry and over the years had developed a friendship. Miles and Prince consulted each other on different musical projects. I remember my father telling me that he wanted to do a studio album with Prince, but, like the Hendrix collaboration, it never materialized. Miles performed with Prince at Paisley Park on New Year's Eve. Their 1987 live onstage collaboration was recorded but was never officially released as far as I know.

CHAPTER ELEVEN

Kind of Blue
(*Columbia, 1959*)

Miles Becomes a Woman Beater

WHILE ONE BYPRODUCT OF USING COCAINE was to draw young women to him, it also turned my father into a misogynist. These young chicks became like beggars wanting to get into his pocketbook and his drugs, but my father thought they were all in love with him. Whenever that didn't turn out to be true, he'd become a woman-beater.

Attacking a Model

This side came out of him one night when he got upset with a young African-American dancer and model who was his latest girlfriend. This was when he was living in the townhouse he had purchased back in 1959 on 77th Street, and I was with him that afternoon.

The girl was beautiful but, as usual, Miles expected too much of her—more than she could give. He expected her to be reliable and loyal, but she was only with him for who he was and his money, not because she was in love with him. She also wanted to move on and date a guy that had more money and prestige than my father did.

I think Miles was also pissed at her because he suspected that she was behind him getting beat up in the vestibule of his building one day. It had something to do with her boyfriend not liking the idea that she was dating Miles.

One day Miles went to answer the door, and these two guys knocked him to the ground and started kicking at him. I wasn't around when that happened. I was living in Chicago getting ready for college. But that's what I heard.

I was there that day with him and her standing in the living room, and I remember Miles got physically abusive with her. He snapped. He figured that he spent thousands of dollars on this broad, getting her high, and couldn't even depend on her. Miles was even paying her rent in his own building.

So his misogynistic temper came out and he threw a broken, jagged drumstick at her. The stick sliced her face. I was shocked. I stood there just shaking my head and hoping he wouldn't go any further.

I tried to calm him down and give the girl some assistance. Miles gave her money for a one-way ticket home, and then he kicked her out of the apartment.

The Castle on 77th Street

What my father did during this "hiatus" when he wasn't busy chasing young women, doing cocaine, or drinking, was listen to Bartók, Spanish flamenco music, and Stravinsky.

He was trying to get his head together about what he wanted to play next. Miles had never given up on music. He was just, as he put it, "doin' some research." But the research sure included lots of drugs, so each day he became more and more like Dr. Jekyll and Mr. Hyde.

Miles was like Dr. Jekyll when it came to music, studying it and doing exciting research about what fresh ideas he'd like to develop. But he was a Mr. Hyde in the way he was killing himself with cocaine. In a lot of ways my father was like Freud, who was also a genius and became addicted to drugs.

I was with him all through those dark days. I was about 30 years old at the time, living in my father's brownstone in a little studio apartment upstairs, right under the roof.

I had to climb five flights of stairs to get to it. There was one little kitchen, a bathroom, and a room about the size of a postage stamp.

Miles had me acting as kind of a janitor for the building. I used to sweep, mop, and wax it all, from the top down, for my father, and collect the rent from the other tenants who lived there.

People were always late with their rent. and I wish Miles had hired a real estate company to do this, because it was really a hassle and I didn't want to be bothered with that. But I did it for him.

Whenever I complained, Miles used to tell me, "You should do it, 'cause it's gonna be yours someday." Of course that never happened. It was just another one of my father's many lies. But I sure wish it had. That building's prime real estate and today it's worth millions.

Miles had a duplex downstairs on the main floor. It was beautiful and looked like a castle with stucco and archways. It had walls that curved because my father didn't like hidden corners. He thought spirits would hide out there.

There was a large wooden table in the kitchen and the windows went from the floor to the ceiling. My father also had a backyard that was mostly made of stone and contained some kind of a sculpture.

Miles used to rehearse on the first floor in a long living room. In the back of the living room he had a custom kitchen with a buffet wheel. The counters all had Formica tops, the cabinets were of expensive wood, and there was a large bathroom. There was even a gym in the basement.

On the second floor there were bedrooms plus a two-level living room with red carpets. I also remember we had this big bathtub with blue tiles.

There used to be a bedroom for us kids when we stayed with him, but somewhere along the line Miles knocked it out and made it into one room with a piano and all his plaques and awards hanging on the walls.

Years later, when my sister Cheryl got married and had a baby, Miles temporarily let them live in a vacant apartment on the second floor. He said, "Yeah, you can stay there until you get on your feet."

It was a long way from his 57th Street apartment, but now my father could afford it because of the incident outside Birdland he was involved in that got him a huge settlement.

You're under Arrest

I was living in Brooklyn at the time, and kind of young—about 12 or 13—and although my mother knew all about it she never mentioned it to me. I found out all about it later on when I read an article in *Jet* magazine that described what had happened.

This was the old Birdland jazz club on 52nd Street and Broadway. Miles was working there with his quintet, and his usual custom was to take a breather between sets. He'd go outside to get some fresh air, relax, and smoke a cigarette.

It was a hot August night in 1958 or 1959, and on this particular night one of his White girlfriends had come to see him. Miles was putting her in a cab when this plainclothes detective saw it. This cop must've been a racist or something, because he walked over to my father and said, "Whatta you doing? You're loitering!"

And here's a Black man with a suit on, not some derelict. Miles tried to tell the cop that he was working there, and that this was a friend he was putting into the cab. He was being polite and not Milesish at all.

Well, this policeman takes out his billy club and knocks my father over the head. The ambulance came and they took him off to jail. The upshot of the whole thing is that it wound up in court and Miles walked away with a $100,000 settlement.

My father put his business sense together and bought the townhouse with that money. It was an old Russian Orthodox church, which he fixed up into a duplex with five apartments over it on the other floors.

He renovated the building so that it had an Arabic look to it. It was beautiful, with a red tile roof and rooms that had lots of stone and wood. Whenever someone was doing a story on him, the photographers would come over and take shots of the building.

It was also just around this time that Miles married Frances Taylor, so my mother felt she didn't need to worry about him anymore. She thought that the marriage would bring him back down to earth, so she left us kids to live there and moved back to St. Louis.

Seeing More of Mr. Hyde

My father had a complex personality to start with, and when he got high it changed for the worse. Drugs enhance what your subconscious is really into. If you've had a bad day and you take some drugs or alcohol, you're going to be mean. And that was Miles. If he had a nice day, he was nice. If he didn't and was on drugs, he'd be mean and rotten.

The more drugs he took the more stupid he became. The more incoherent he was, the more his libido would come out, and then Miles would get into some freaky kind of activity with a female.

When he'd start taking the cocaine he was in a good mood, but when he increased his indulgence his mood would change into the Mr. Hyde state of mind. He'd get short-tempered at those girls that came over there when he realized that all they wanted from him was his drugs.

My father would confuse friendship and love. Miles would fall in love with them like he did with the model he attacked, but they wouldn't fall back in love with him. They were just trying to use him for what he had. They may have liked him or something, but it sure wasn't love.

As I said, my father expected that these women should be more loyal or something, and they weren't even thinking like that. You don't pick a woman who's also doing drugs to be your loyal companion, and then when she goes and does something wrong you get depressed and everything.

But that's the way he was. Miles was a very sensitive person when he thought somebody had done him wrong—and then he would become violent. But what did he expect out of a girl who just wanted to be with him to get high? And when he was out of drugs, all she wanted was for him to get more—even though they'd be doing this shit all night.

This kind of woman wasn't looking after my father's health or in love with him. Then when someone told Miles that she did something or that she was with another man, he'd get all depressed and angry about it and slap them around and stuff like that.

Kinky Sex with My Wife?

Miles was so out of control at times with his drugs that once, back in the '70s when I was married and had a child of my own, he even suggested that me, my wife Carol, and he all have some kinky sex.

Carol was a graduate of Howard University as an English major. She was a very pretty brown-skinned Jamaican girl and quite intelligent. Miles one night got so high on coke that he didn't know what he was doing. When he was like that he'd look at a woman like she was nothing more than a sex object.

He said to me, "Come on, bring Carol down here. I have this other one here with a big butt, you know, and we can do some freaky stuff together." I was pretty shocked. I mean, I would never get into something like that. It wasn't something I ever thought about doing and I sure wouldn't do it with the mother of my children.

I rejected that idea right away and looked at him like he was nuts. He really didn't even seem to care. His attitude was always very selfish. I

mean, what kind of morals and principles did he have to suggest something like this?

I knew he wasn't raised without moral values. My grandfather had strict
morals and principles. He firmly believed that a son should go to college
and provide for his family. That's why he sent Miles to Juilliard in the first
place, even though he didn't totally approve of his son's course of study.

Somewhere along the line Miles had lost sight of those values. So what
happened that night really upset me. I didn't like that idea coming out of
him. It was a Mr. Hyde thought, because this is something that Mr. Hyde
would think about doing—having sex with his son's wife.

He Had Demons inside Himself

As the years passed, I became very disappointed with my father's behavior.
I was like *his* father, trying to stand him up straight and get him not to
indulge too much. But he couldn't stop. When you do drugs, you become
their victim.

I stayed with him only because I didn't want my father to be a victim of
himself or of anyone else. I didn't want him to make himself an easy target
for people who wanted to rob him, or cheat him out of his money, or harm
him because they saw that he was too stoned to focus.

These women of his were always trying to beat Miles out of his money.
They were only hanging around him for what he had: money and drugs.
Miles always had them around for their beauty—and they knew they were
beautiful—but they had no loyalty to him. They just wanted to drain him
of what he had, and then they'd walk away and move on to the next guy.

Then he'd get depressed and I would try to cheer him up and console
him in some kind of way. Sure, there were people who loved him and everything like that, but when he started befriending drug dealers and females
who had no principles or morals, he was more likely to be ripped off.

I couldn't stop him from going outside and getting more drugs short
of knocking him out or chaining him up like his father did. So I said to
myself, "Well, I just have to support him and see that nothing bad happens to him."

I remember always saying to him, "Why do you need more of this stuff?
Slow down. You don't need any more." But he'd still want to do more of it.

He wouldn't give me any explanation. He'd just whistle up at me at three or four o'clock in the morning when I was living upstairs. I'd come running down and he'd say to me in that hoarse voice of his, "Let's go."

I'd say, "Where ya goin'?"

He'd say, "Come on, let's go."

So we'd take a cab and he'd go see somebody to buy drugs from. He had demons inside that were torturing him, and he couldn't sit still.

Maybe the demons had something to do with his mother—my grandmother. From what I heard she was very mean to him and my grandfather was unable to stop all her abuse.

I wasn't even born yet, but a close friend of the family told me that Miles's mother was that way because she was upset that he and his brother, Vernon, were born too dark-skinned.

At the time that's how Black people thought. They wanted their kids to be a high-yellow color of skin—to be half White or whatever—so she was disappointed and angry about it.

According to the story, almost anything that Miles did that upset my grandmother, she'd yell, "I'm gonna beat the hell out of you—wait till I catch you." And Miles would run into the closet somewhere and hide.

My grandmother would go looking for him, yelling, "I'm comin' and I'm gonna get your Black ass." The thing is that despite such treatment, Miles still loved the hell out of his mother.

I don't remember my grandmother ever being mean to me, but my father's sister—my Aunt Dorothy May—was also a bitch, and so was my sister for whatever her reasons were. These were the two who successfully conspired to cut me out of Miles's will, which I'll talk about more later.

Anyway, that's what I was told about my father's upbringing. And if it's true, then it's a clear case of abuse. Whether or not Miles did something wrong, I don't think she needed to beat him. But I think that a lot of African-American women both then and now are confused about who they are, and my grandmother was one of them.

My grandfather loved his wife and didn't want to lose her. So he couldn't really stop it. They used to argue a lot, but she'd have her way. Most of the time my grandfather wasn't at home because he was out of the house working, so there was no way he could stop her from that kind of abuse.

I think that's a big part of the reason why Miles had demons in him and why he abused his girlfriends and other people as well. I loved my grandmother, but I also know, having received a master's degree in psychotherapy, that what she did to him as a kid stayed with him and that he later on transferred her behavior towards the women in his life. The earlier in life anything like that happens—any kind of psychological trauma—the worse it is. And it comes back to haunt you when you're an adult.

I Became His Bodyguard

I began to escort Miles around town—I had to. He was my father. What else could I do short of chaining him up and putting a lock on the door? I became his bodyguard and had to risk my own life because Miles was running around and acting like a fool. Who else could he trust to keep him out of harm's way but the son he had raised to respect and love him?

I remember one time when he went to see someone to check out what kind of drugs they had. He ended up staying there snorting it all up. Then he paid for the drugs with, of all things, a traveler's check.

Well, needless to say, this dealer's out there to get cash, and he got pissed at being handed a check instead of dollar bills. It was only my presence that kept my father from getting hurt and robbed.

Miles said to this guy, "Hey, come by tomorrow morning and I'll make sure the money's alright." When we left there, I'm not sure my father understood, but I certainly did, about how close he had come to getting his ass kicked or even killed.

There was another time when he went into some place and started arguing with some dealer about drugs. This guy wanted to manhandle him, so I just knocked the guy out. I was in shape back then, because I'd been doing some boxing.

Once I was with Miles and he walked into this bar on 72nd Street off of Broadway called the Only Child to score some drugs. He got into an argument with the dealer and called him a name.

Well, that hurt the man's feelings and he got angry with my father and wanted to get up and push him around. I couldn't allow that, being right there with him, so I had to stop it. I had to cold-cock him too.

I mean, that's how stupid my father could be. He had just had a hip operation and he goes into this place and calls this guy, "You muthafucka, you bitch," you this and that. And this guy's sitting down with two women and he's high and he got up and tried to manhandle Miles.

My father would always be going to different places to get out of the house and have a drink or something. Like I said, he was a fish out of water when he wasn't working or playing, and needed that exhilaration. He seemed to need some kind of excitement that gave him a spark.

Miles would get arrogant with people and they would react in different ways—sometimes really angry—but my father often wasn't serious about his attitude. It was kind of like an act. He was playing with people. But people would take him seriously and then he'd wonder why they would get so mad and want to punch him out.

I'd say, "You just called that man a bitch or something—you called him a name. What the hell did you expect?"

Miles would just shrug his shoulders and with an innocent expression on his face ask, "What did I do?" I'd say, "Don't you see what you just did?" He knew what he had done. My father was pulling my leg. He liked to jerk people's strings.

I Became His Home Attendant Too

I was more than just my father's bodyguard. I was sometimes his nurse and home attendant too. I recall one time when he was on tour in San Francisco, and I was with him. I had to take him to the hospital when he got really dehydrated from the cocaine.

I was in my hotel room at the time, and he called me on the phone sounding very sick. I immediately raced downstairs to his room, picked him up in his pajamas, put him on my back, and caught a cab to Peninsula Hospital. They put tubes into him because his electrolyte count was way down.

This incident was on top of all the other medical problems he suffered from at the time—sickle-cell anemia, ulcers, bursitis, bad heart, and God knows what else. When he got out of the hospital I had to act as his home aid. It wasn't the first time that I had to be his nurse or his home attendant.

A Great Miles Story

My father couldn't stop laughing as he told me this story.

Miles was at home in his 77th Street duplex, and his second-floor space didn't have any burglar bars on the windows. So one day this burglar thought he could get in.

My father saw the guy breaking in and he's on the phone with the police. When the police got there, my father said, "Yeah, he's still upstairs."

The police found the guy sitting there and looking like he was a guest in the house so that he wouldn't appear guilty. He was just sitting there drinking a bottle of Heineken.

What was so funny is that my father had been drinking these Heineken beers and pissing into the empty bottles because he'd kicked back and was too lazy to go to the bathroom. So you know what the "guest" was drinking. . . .

Seeing Spirits

Miles had dope that was so strong, he'd sometimes flush it down the toilet because he was scared of it himself. It caused him to start seeing and hearing things and, at one point, he even started talking to the spirits of Coltrane, Monk, and the Bird, who had all died years earlier.

Not only that, but when he'd get high Miles would also talk to the "haunts" of his mother and father and anybody and anything else he wanted to talk to; he'd even talk to the bugs in his house and give them names.

I remember my father saying to me in that whisper voice of his, "Hey, come over here. You hear that?" And I'd know that he was delusional, but I had to play the game. So I'd come over and he'd be saying, "You hear that?"

And finally I'd say, "I don't hear nothin'. What're you doin'?"

He'd say, "Okay, okay, man, I don't hear nothin'."

But I knew he was hearing those haunts.

No Limit When It Came to Staying High

You know, when people get inebriated or high they start acting silly. Cocaine can do that to you. At first, though, it makes your senses very sharp. It takes away your appetite and makes your hearing very sensitive. It also heightens your libido.

But then, after a while, you get diminishing effects. It's a drug that keeps you trying to get that original high. But you really can't do so until the next day or two days afterwards, no matter how much more you take.

Your brain can only take so much of that pleasure all at once. It's like you have sex with a woman and you reach a climax, then you have to rest. That's how cocaine is.

When you can't get that original high, it makes you idiotic. You run around trying to buy more and more of it, and then you use more of it trying to get there. It's like you become desperate to reach that peak of pleasure again—and that's how my father sometimes was.

What you really need to do is take a break—dry out for a few hours or a day or so and then go back to it. Otherwise you're just acting silly and wasting your money. And coke is a very expensive drug.

My father told me what it cost him. One time he said, "This is a rich man's habit." Miles would spend three hundred dollars, five hundred dollars, 15 hundred dollars, depending on whether he wanted to buy an "eight ball" or a smaller amount.

Miles was just one of those people who don't know how to take drugs in moderation or drink in moderation. He said he did, but he really didn't. It was almost impossible for him to be moderate in anything, from his music to his pursuits of pleasure.

Putting You Out on a Limb

My father would expect you to do something for him, but he wouldn't give you the resources to do it. He expected you to pick it up from nowhere, and sometimes it was virtually impossible for you to do so. He would put you out on a limb, leave you there, and see if you could climb back.

For example, I came to New York specifically to help him. We were supposed to be helping each other. I had some problems of my own, but I was also trying to go to Kennedy-King College in Chicago at the time—I had a scholarship to go there.

Then one day Pete Cosey, the guitar player that was working with him at the time, called me and said, "Your father really needs you. Maybe you can help each other."

This was just after his run-in with the two guys who beat him up in the hallway of his apartment building, and it made me feel bad when I heard that. So I went to New York, and my father let me stay in that studio apartment. But what was I supposed to do for money?

I mean, I had aspirations of going to college at that time, and I had to put those plans on hold. I didn't want to be dependent on my father, although he was kind enough to give me dinner, lend me some money, or whatever.

Sure, I had my studio up there, but I wanted to be independent and on my own. God wants you to have a life of your own too, and I didn't just want to go on being my father's escort and bodyguard.

So I had to go out and get a temporary job through a temp agency—any kind of job that I could take so that I had money to live on. Eventually I went to the Manhattan School of Music and took a couple of courses in music theory that Miles paid for.

The rest of my time was spent being at my father's beck and call. I really couldn't have the kind of life that I wanted. He was so overwhelming as a person, being the genius that he was and being my father, that I just couldn't say no to him.

When I came to New York and saw the expensive lifestyle my father was living, I wanted to create a life like that for myself. I'd been raised around Ferraris, and fine clothes, and had expensive tastes. But being around him all the time I had nothing to build on to reach my goal.

Later on in life, when I had just come out of the army, I remember my father telling me one thing that was very positive. He said, "You've served your country, now go do something for yourself." He meant I should go to school and make a success out of myself. And that's what I really wanted to do I was already accepted into Kennedy-King.

Instead I went to New York City to be with my father because he needed me there. There I was out on a limb with nothing to hold on to.

My Little Brother Slaps My Father

Nobody else in my family but me wanted to put up with Miles's attitude. I was always trying to get my father, me, and my younger brother together, but Miles would never want to do it because one time my brother in a messed-up state of mind had slapped him. It had to do with Squeaky not bringing my father something that he wanted. I always tried to tell my father, "Well, he wasn't himself. He was sick." Squeaky was out there trying to be like his fathers but he just couldn't pull it off.

That's another example of what I mean about my father putting you out on a limb and leaving you there. Miles showed my younger brother his lifestyle of drugs, women, fine clothes, and the rest of the good life.

The "good life" part of it was okay because Miles wanted us kids to live as well as he did. I remember him once saying, "I want my kids to have the same." But at the same time, he was doing the drug thing and demonstrating to us that it was the icing on the cake.

What kind of example was that? My brother picked up on it, but he just wasn't ready for that kind of fast lifestyle and to be another Miles. He was too young. What Squeaky really needed was an education, not a course in drugs and wild women. That's the kind of ideas Miles should have been putting into my brother's head—pushing him to become some kind of professional person and not to show him all this high-rolling stuff.

Still, I know it wasn't something my father really did on purpose. As I said, Miles always wanted the best for us. He would always buy us encyclopedias and encourage us to educate ourselves and to do good things. But he didn't set a good example.

So there was my brother trying to imitate my father's lifestyle, and he overdid it.

Then there was that day that Squeaky slapped him. My father got pissed and my brother was gone. Squeaky's pockets were now empty because Miles was mad at him and it was my father who always kept them filled with money.

As much as he wanted to, my younger brother could no longer support himself with that kind of lifestyle. Like me, he also found himself out on a limb.

I'm glad the drugs didn't get to me to that extent. Even though I was with my father a lot when he was hitting the pavement on his drug sojourns, sometimes I was with him when he was doing his thing.

Sure, I tried it and did it for a while, but I was never affected by drugs to the point that I was dependent on drugs. I never wanted drugs to be the big part of my lifestyle. That's why I didn't keep it up—only my father did. Cocaine was a way of life for my father, but it wasn't for me.

CHAPTER TWELVE

Miles Ahead
(Columbia, 1957)

Getting Furious with Betty Davis

BESIDES TRYING TO MAKE SURE my father didn't get hurt when he was making the rounds doing drug buys, I often traveled with him when he was on tour. I was his road manager and used to hold the money after each performance and pay the band off.

I remember once in 1973, we took off on tour and traveled all over the country in a limousine. His manager had rented the limo to take us to Cincinnati, San Francisco, Philadelphia, Washington, Boston, and Chicago.

There are a couple of things I recall about that tour. I remember that in Washington, D.C., we were staying in the same hotel as Richard Pryor. Richard used to have an apartment in my father's townhouse on West 77th Street.

Richard, who had a lot of drug problems of his own, wanted me to go to a party he was having in the hotel. I said, "No, I gotta be available for my father." I didn't want to go to a party and indulge in drugs and then not be ready for whatever Miles might need me for.

I don't think Richard much liked me for turning down his invitation, but the whole time I traveled with my father I was like a soldier on a mission to keep him safe. And I did my job well.

I did it out of love and respect. My father trusted me and I was reliable, and I wanted to remain that way. And if that meant not going to a party or missing some other kind of fun, staying straight for Miles was my first priority.

In Boston, there was a day when my father grew angry with a young woman, Betty Mabry Davis, another one of his wives. She was a funky, raunchy singer but I always thought of her more as a high-class groupie than a singer. My father had fallen head over heels for her as he did for most of his women.

But despite his feelings for her, Miles got really furious when he learned that his manager was letting Betty use some of his equipment—like his keyboard and his speakers—that was supposed to be in storage.

I think behind his anger was that my father suspected something was going on between Betty and his manager. There were also rumors of an affair with Jimi Hendrix. Things like that really affected him because, like I said, Miles was very sensitive to what people did, especially if he thought someone he expected more loyalty from didn't live up to his expectations.

And now he surmised that Betty hadn't. Also, he and Betty were going through some kind of split or something at the time, so all of that played on my father's mind.

When Miles found out about the unauthorized use of his equipment, he blew his top. He told his manager right away, "Look, I want an inventory of all my equipment. I didn't tell Betty that she could use this or that. So why are you letting her use that?"

That wasn't supposed to happen. My father was supposed to have been notified or asked about the use of his equipment, and he didn't appreciate things being done in this underhanded way.

Miles completed his gig, but not before he angrily demanded that his manager give him an advance on the money he was supposed to be paid, and then later fired him.

This episode ruined our stay in Boston. All Miles wanted to talk about was his "betrayal" by his wife and his manager. Within one year of getting married, Betty and Miles called it quits, although she continued to record under the name Betty Davis.

I Enjoyed Being with My Father

Despite what had happened in Boston, I enjoyed that tour, sitting in the back seat of the limo and just being alone with my father. It was a precious time when you can be with somebody you care about—especially your father. I'd been going through good times and bad times with Miles, and I still remember that this was one of the good times.

It was a rare moment when we could bond. We were together eight hours a day as the car sped through America and just talked like a normal father and son. Miles told me some things about the horn and this and that—just little small-talk stuff. We did a lot of relating to each other on that trip. I mean, there we were, the two of us—no women or anything. Just father and son enjoying each other's company.

On one tour, I remember a funny story about Toronto. We caught a plane that got us and the band into the Toronto airport. At customs, the inspectors were looking for drugs, of course.

They were searching the guitar cases and all that, and finally Miles got annoyed and said to them, "I don't care nothin' 'bout that uniform you've got on. We're bringing your country some music. Leave my musicians alone, they don't have nothin' they're not supposed to have."

The inspectors laughed and found out pretty quickly who my father was—a couple of them being Miles Davis fans themselves. They let us all pass without any further ado, but not before collecting a couple of autographs from my father.

Miles Was a Liar

My father lied to me about quite a few things over the years, but it was the townhouse he owned on West 77th Street which still gets to me today—how he deceived me about that.

Me and my siblings always thought that this former church property would stay in the family. Miles always told us that we would own the building after he died. But he had other plans.

I remember how he always wanted his building to look nice so that he could rent apartments. If it wasn't clean enough he'd tell me, "Gregory, do the stairs," or something like that. I'd do it and he'd give me a little money for my allowance. Then he'd say, "You should be doin' it for nothin', 'cause it's gonna be yours one of these days."

But like I said, that was a lie. Instead, he sold it. All the promises Miles made about that building went out the window.

My father was like a chameleon. I'd just expect almost anything out of him anytime. It was the drugs that made him change like that. When my father was high, he didn't know what he was doing or just didn't care about the consequences.

One day he'd love you and the next day he'd decide, "I don't like any of my kids anymore." One day he's promising you a building. The next day he's thinking something entirely different.

In most families, especially well-to-do families, things are supposed to be set in concrete—especially financial plans for your children's future.

If you don't set these things in concrete, or delegate important decisions to others, it can rip apart a family. The townhouse was sold right out from under us because Miles thought he needed money.

I think he acted on bad advice from Cicely Tyson, who he was dating at the time and later married. All I know is that if Miles needed money, all he had to do was put his horn to his mouth.

But he got to the point where he had done all these drugs and, as a result, had become so selfish that he decided he didn't want to pay taxes anymore on his property so he'd get rid of it. Cicely probably encouraged my father to do so, because it seemed to me she wasn't all that concerned about the future needs of his kids.

My father was also having trouble with his tenants in the 77th Street townhouse. Perhaps, if Miles had stayed clean, he'd have managed the building better.

Cicely Tyson Cleans House

Cicely Tyson started running Miles's life. She called it "cleaning house." Among the things she did was clean out all my boxing trophies, plaques, and awards I had sweated blood to win and had proudly presented to my father. One day I found all those trophies gone.

Then, as part of her "cleaning house," she told my father which people he shouldn't be seeing, saying they were all part of his drug problem. I know that she also encouraged Miles to sell the house where a lot of my memories were.

I guess getting rid of the building and the friends she didn't approve of was part of her Miles Davis cleanup project. But what kind of cleanup project was that?

My father took all her advice because he had developed this "I don't give a fuck" kind of attitude. But you can't have that kind of attitude and be a good father.

Although Miles didn't seem to care about our futures, my mother certainly did. But she didn't have any kind of authority with my father because they were divorced. He wouldn't listen to her about the building or anything else.

I mean they would talk—they weren't really angry with each other—but he was a knucklehead. Miles was just very stubborn. My mother asked him not to sell the building for the sake of the kids. Her pleas fell on deaf ears. By 1989, Miles and Cicely's marriage was over, and home for Miles became Malibu—not New York City.

Family Feuds

As I've already mentioned, around this time my father wasn't talking to my younger brother because of that slapping incident. According to my mother, Miles IV had slapped him. My Aunt Dorothy just loved it when Miles and his sons split or fought. I believe she was doing her best to have her own son, Vincent, become Miles's surrogate son.

Rumor was that Dorothy would always be instigating against me and Little Miles in favor of her son. She would, for example, always be pushing Miles to have her son, Vincent, play in his band and nobody else—including me. She also used to visit from Chicago when my father was sick, but I believe it wasn't out of any real concern. Despite the rosy picture that other books have painted, I think it was largely pretense. In my opinion she really wanted to know if my father was dying so that she could get involved in his will.

Vincent eventually did end up playing drums for a while in Miles's band. He was a nice kid. I watched him grow up until his high school years, and when he was a child I even used to babysit for him. I still remember how I would sit him down on a set of drums to distract him and keep him from crying.

Somehow he wound up in Miles's will. When I was around, he never seemed particularly close to my father although he was recruited into the family business and appeared on some of Miles's sessions.

There was a lot of intrigue going on in my family when it came to my father's money, starting with how I suspect my aunt helped to influence his will as far back as three years before he died—a will he signed, but never read.

When they gathered around Miles when he was in and out of a coma, they seemed to me like vultures. While I had come to my father for money over the years, I never looked at my father like a piece of meat.

What I did for my father I did from my heart out of love and respect. And I always thought he'd have sense enough to do the right thing for me and my brother. A will can express love and gratitude. I know Miles loved me. He had no real score to settle.

Never did I imagine that Miles would leave his two sons out of his will—especially after all I'd been through with him. I had put my life on hold just to be by his side through all his craziness.

You know, blood's supposed to be thicker than water. But I guess when it comes to money that's not always the case.

Despite Everything, Miles Still Had a Good Side

It's true that as my father grew more and more famous, he was doing more and more drugs and acting crazy. But he still had a good side; he just didn't know what he was doing when he was high.

Even when Miles wasn't on drugs he became more selfish and self-centered, sometimes more concerned about himself than his children. But I always sensed that there was more to the man than that; I knew buried deep within him there was the good part of his soul. My father simply became a victim of his own drug abuse.

It had come to the point when his night life blotted out his daytime life, because the demons come out at night and my father had plenty of them. Miles had become almost schizophrenic, no longer knowing who he really was.

But even as I observed him at some of his worst moments, I remembered the Miles Davis of my childhood. I recalled the early days before he began indulging in drugs and his mind wasn't as twisted as it now was.

Thinking back about those years, I remembered Miles as a good guy, a father with a tender heart who would take us kids to ballgames, buy clothes for us, and really care. My father loved the hell out of me, and when I was a baby we even used to take baths together. Back then I really looked up to him.

Miles had spent money teaching me how to box and even provided me with a personal trainer. He sent me to the best schools and really was a father to me. I remembered all that even when drugs became the center of his existence and his jovial personality changed to that of a sinister Mr. Hyde.

Today, when I think about it, I know that Miles was indulging in drugs because he wanted to build another world. He had decided that his normal life was not what he wanted it to be.

Or maybe something stuck in his subconscious that was responsible for him becoming a changeling, especially because of the way his mother had beaten the hell out of him when he was young.

Despite all of his unsettling behavior, I stuck with my father through thick and thin. Although I couldn't afford to go see him when he was dying, I was there in spirit. I had never abandoned him.

CHAPTER THIRTEEN

We Want Miles
(Columbia, 1981)

His Retirement Is Over

BY 1980, MY FATHER WAS BACK in the studio, recording. It was a bittersweet year for my father because his good friends Charles Mingus and Bill Evans had both died and he was broken up over it. However, at the same time, he produced a great album, *The Man with the Horn*.

That year Miles also recorded pop tunes by artists like Kenny Loggins and Cyndi Lauper. He loved her song "Time After Time" and didn't give a damn what his critics might think about his playing ballads again.

I think it was a private joke—acknowledging the public demand that he return to performing—that Miles also put out a record called *We Want Miles*. This was his answer to people asking all the time, "Where's Miles?"

Miles was like a fish out of water sitting at home, and he just needed to perform. His creative juices were starting to flow again, and the music he was putting out sounded better and better to him. My father was in the zone again. He knew which way he wanted to go.

Miles Gets Diabetes

I mentioned earlier how many physical ailments my father suffered from— everything from sickle-cell anemia to a broken hip. Miles was prone to getting pneumonia, which he first got back in the 1940s walking around the streets of New York high on drugs and without an overcoat.

Adding to that, he was psychologically sick from battling all the demons that were inside tormenting him. But the resurgence of his creative ideas overcame his health problems. The music kept him busy and went a long way to vanquishing his demons and keeping his mind off his physical ailments.

Then in 1981 his medical problems got worse when my father suffered a diabetic stroke. It affected one side of his body, especially his right hand. But he was a remarkable man.

Incredibly enough, Miles was able to come out of that and play like nothing bothered him at all. His audiences couldn't even detect that anything was wrong, especially in his trumpet playing. It was simply amazing!

When I was on the road with him I knew how sick he was. At times when he was onstage he'd even cough up some blood and all the mucus he had in his body from the drugs he was taking. But Miles would still play a gig to the end and do fantastic stuff with his horn.

I remember once on Ramadan, the Muslim holy fast days that I celebrate, that my father fasted. Afterwards, he told me, "Rahman, I tried it and you should've seen all the stuff that came out of me." (Rahman, by the way, is the Muslim name I chose after I declared my faith in Islam.)

It truly amazed me how my father worked through all his physical ailments. I know people who've had strokes, and they walk funny and sometimes they don't have use of their hands or arms.

But Miles didn't have any of that. It was really incredible to see him play at such a professional level because I knew how sick he was—I'd spend nights with him being his nurse.

I remember after a while saying to myself, "He's got more than just this physical attraction to that horn and that music. He's got something else that's giving him this strength—some God-given gift."

Miles had inside him what every great artist has—some unexplainable energy. It was his destiny to play his music, and he possessed some kind of amazing willpower to do so.

Unless he was in the hospital, my father never missed a performance. He was able to make every session and not even miss a note—even when a session was three hours long!

Sometimes during the breaks his roadies would have to give him some oxygen backstage in his dressing room. Once, at Carnegie Hall, they had to carry him off the stage when he finished playing and immediately give him oxygen. He had given everything he had.

That stroke, however, didn't stop him from still using any kind of drug that people would hand him during a concert. You know, when you become

famous or the greatest, people will hand you anything, and Miles was trying everything they gave him.

I always would ask him, "What are you doin'? You don't know this person
who gave you this stuff. It might be dish powder." But Miles didn't care.
He'd snort it or pop it or whatever.

Marrying Cicely Tyson

In 1966 Cicely did a movie called *A Man Named Adam*. It was loosely
based on my father's life. Sammy Davis, Jr., played Miles. Sammy later
became one of my father's best friends.

Sammy, by the way, had some of the same conflicts that my father had
and so was perfect for the role. Cicely became intrigued with Miles after
that movie, and she made it a point to meet my father.

There was some spark and romance there and they fell in love. They
got married in 1981 at the home of a good friend of my father's—Bill Cosby—who then had a house in Massachusetts. Among the guests were Max
Roach, Dizzy Gillespie, and Dick Gregory.

The only thing I didn't like about the marriage is that my father let Cicely do the "mundane" things that he should have been doing himself. Like
I said earlier, Cicely believed that she was helping Miles clean up his life
by "cleaning house," but in the process she alienated me.

I still resented the fact that she took my trophies that I had won and
convinced my father to get rid of them. And Miles didn't even stop her.
These were things that were very valuable and sentimental to me, but she
didn't know—or care to know—their personal value. My father probably
asked her to clean the house—not to throw out the trophies—but she
couldn't have cared less about my achievements. And Miles had a total
lack of concern for details—except when it came to himself. He turned
everything over to her, and she did what she wanted. But those trophies
represented my sweat and blood. I earned those things. They were boxing
trophies and I had to fight to win them.

Not only did Cicely have these trophies thrown out, she was also sug-
gesting to Miles which friends he should answer the door for and which he
shouldn't. Some of those people were good friends to my father, they weren't
junkies or cocaine sellers. But he listened to her anyway. And why did she

support him in selling the townhouse? She knew that house was really meant for the children. I mean, that's what he worked for—to leave something for his sons—and any woman married to him would know that. What else does a man work for except to take care of his family and children?

You know something, I don't even blame her as much as I do my father. He was a creative genius and his mind was on more artistic matters. Miles delegated. He'd rather have someone else take care of things if it didn't have to do with his music. So he left all these decisions up to Cicely. Some of these decisions still cause me pain today—like throwing away my sports trophies.

Maybe Cicely thought she was helping my father by cleaning house, but what she was really doing was tearing down a house that he'd built over many years—a place the family called home.

Me and Drugs

I didn't like Cicely's attitude towards me. It was during this period that Miles didn't want to see me for a while because he was a little disillusioned and disappointed that I was also indulging in drugs. Ironically, *he* had introduced me and Squeaky to them.

But like I said before, I never got to the point where I was a junkie or anything like that. It just didn't appeal to me that much. It was just a little period in my life—part of the climate of the times when everyone was getting high on something or other.

I think Miles got overly concerned and put too much emphasis on it. Someone probably had told him I was a junkie and he believed it. But that was pure bullshit—a damned lie!

In Miles's autobiography he says I came back from Vietnam a "changed person," and "from then on he cost me a lot of trouble, headaches, and money while he lived with me." But I didn't go to Vietnam. I went to Germany with the 56th Medical Battalion. They went on to Vietnam but I didn't because my tour of duty was over and I got an honorable discharge.

Other books say that I got into trouble and this and that, but it's all bullshit. Everybody gets into trouble—especially if you have a father who was always looking for it and you were his bodyguard. It's a wonder I didn't go crazy trying to be his father rather than him being mine. I was always trying to keep him off drugs and away from the pimps and whores and dope sellers. If I got into any trouble it's because I was doing that and standing up for my father as his bodyguard and trying to protect my family.

Drugs weren't something I wanted to be involved with on a continuing basis—not then, when I was bouncing around the streets of New York with my father acting as his bodyguard, or now.

It just wasn't that bad on my part. I never overdid it and I wasn't making it a lifestyle or anything like that the way Miles had done. I did some drugs for a short period of time before letting it go. My biggest concern was never how I could get more drugs but rather how I could take care of my father

Still, I certainly could understand why my father would get upset. He had enough to think about in getting his own head together without also worrying about me. And to tell you the truth, I needed some time on my own to get my head together too.

He's lucky I didn't have a nervous breakdown from being with him all the time, trying to keep him from killing himself because of all the drugs he was taking, and advising him to lay off—"Whatta'ya doing to yourself? Why do you have to use so much?"

I mean, three or four o'clock in the morning he'd whistle for me and we'd have to go to some after-hours spot for him to pick up a package or something. And then there was this revolving door of drug dealers coming in and out of the house. He was always in danger of one of these drug dealers hurting or killing him—and so was I.

So we decided to take a break from each other. But whatever the feelings were at the time between us, Miles was still my father and I had no hate or animosity towards him. I just didn't want to push myself on him or anybody. I wanted to be alone for a while.

Cicely Keeps Us Apart

I remember that I'd call Miles once in a while just to see how he was doing, and Cicely would tell me my father wasn't available. I wondered why he couldn't deal with the situation himself instead of, once again, relying on someone else to do so.

By now my father had sold his building. Just before he moved to California he was living with Cicely in her apartment somewhere along West End

Avenue. I made some efforts to visit him, but every time I did she'd act like some duke protecting the king.

Instead of saying to Miles, "Hey, Miles, it's your son downstairs and maybe it's important," she'd say he couldn't see me or something like that. I was always blocked by her from seeing or speaking to my father.

As I said before, I don't fault her as much as blame him for letting this happen. Sure, maybe he thought he needed a break from me, but this was personal family business that Miles should have handled on his own, not through an intermediary.

So Cicely always kept me away from my father. She thought I was a bad influence on him, but she was wrong. I wasn't the one influencing him to take drugs, I was the one trying to advise him not to.

It was the ones who were influencing my father to take drugs that Cicely should have kept away from him, not stepping in between the love of a father for his son and a son for his father.

Although I was a young man—much stronger physically than my father—who could take drugs or leave them, still I think it was the love that Miles had for me which caused him to be concerned about my own use of drugs.

Miles and Cicely Split

Miles bought a house in Malibu. The ocean was somewhere in the back of it—at least that's what I was told. I was never there, although I wish I had been.

In California, my father had a different group of people hovering around him. There was my half-brother Erin, who was even younger than Squeaky, and Miles's sister, Dorothy, who presumably was continuing her campaign against me. Even Dorothy's son, Vincent, stayed or visited from time to time. Cicely wasn't there because they had already split even before he moved out west.

Moving out there was good for Miles. It gave him a chance to rest, to recover from his extreme lifestyle. Malibu was warmer, and there was less temptation. He was feeling stronger out there, coping better with all his various health problems—even sometimes swimming in the ocean with his new girlfriend, Jo Gelbard, who I'll tell you more about later.

Miles had his Ferrari. He took everything easy, California style, not like his New York City schedule with rehearsals and this and that. Maybe all this helped him to free his mind of the demons that he'd left behind in New York—the demons that he himself had created.

I'm not exactly sure why he and Cicely had split. They had just grown apart and then finally separated. She was a great actress and had a lot of work to do, and Miles was a great musician who also was busy all the time.

They were two people with strong personalities and active careers. When you're on top of your career, and you're dealing with a woman who's on top of her career, it's inevitable that you're going to have some kind of conflict going on.

I'm sure the drugs played a big role in their separation too. It was always the drugs that made Miles delusional and jealous, suspicious and angry towards the women in his life. I don't know why it would be any different with Cicely.

Miles Was a Sensitive Person

My father was a very sensitive person and I remember how saddened he was over the deaths of his good friends like Charlie Mingus. He was also really broken up when Duke Ellington died in 1974, Miles loved and cared about the Duke. When Duke was lying in a hospital dying, I said, "Why don't you go see him?"

He said, "Nah, a man like that, he wouldn't want me to see him like that." He remembered Duke being so sharp and well-dressed. It was the same kind of feeling he had toward his mother and father. Miles wouldn't go to their funerals either. He just wanted to remember important people in his life as he once knew them, or, maybe he couldn't deal with death—theirs or the thought of his own.

Switching from Columbia to Warners

There are a lot of versions out there about why Miles switched from his long-time relationship with Columbia Records to Warner Bros. This happened just around the time when he sold his house at 312 West 77th Street and had decided to move out to Malibu.

The inside story I heard is that Miles sold the West 77th Street building to pay back Columbia Records. They were seriously pressuring him at the time about money they claimed they had advanced him and that he owed them.

They also felt they had invested a lot of money to market him, but Miles had fooled around—his retirement and other stuff—and so had breached his contract.

Columbia was not without fault. My father thought they weren't doing a good job in marketing him, and he also felt that they weren't giving him a chance to grow as an artist. The only thing they wanted was for him to play his horn all the time.

Miles saw himself differently. He was more than just a horn player. My father felt that he was also a composer and an avant-garde musician, meaning that he was always looking for new directions in his music and he wanted his record company to support all his talents.

But Columbia just didn't understand that. To them he was Miles Davis the jazz artist, period. They didn't want him to play the organ or the keyboard that he always had whenever he appeared onstage. Even when he recorded he sometimes wanted to lay down some chords, but they wanted him to specifically be sweating over his horn.

It was the same old racial stereotype. They thought a Black man should only be sweating over his horn and look like he's really working. And he was down with that and into other musical things besides just his horn.

So it was a combination of things that led to the breakup: the way they were treating him, his need for money because of the financial pressure Columbia was putting on him, and also because Miles really didn't care about making records at the time—he was trying to get his addiction under control, like he had done with heroin.

It just came to a point where they couldn't reconcile their differences, and Miles decided to switch to Warners to make a new start. All he had to do was put that horn to his mouth and someone was sure to pick him up anyway, so he didn't feel at all anxious about leaving his longtime record company.

The biggest thing behind the switch is that my father just didn't like being stuck to a microphone. Columbia wanted him standing up, fused to a microphone and sweating over it, but that was an old idea that. Miles wanted to break. The switch to Warner gave him a chance to do that He had a more liberal contract with them that allowed him to have a wireless mike and walk around, which gave him more air and less sweat. He didn't want to be another Satchmo.

Michael Jackson, Prince, Sammy Davis, and Some Others

Michael Jackson was one of many musicians who appreciated my father's artistry, and Miles dug his style of performing too. He thought that Michael was a rare breed.

Miles especially thought that Prince was a genius, and the same with James Brown. My father was also listening to a lot of rap music at the time, and really liked the rapper Easy Mo Bee. One of his last albums was a session in which he collaborated with him.

My father liked any kind of music that had a message, and that included hip-hop and rap, even at a time when it wasn't as popular as it is today. He even loved ballet as a musical form and thought he could add something to it in his own creative way.

Another performer my father really liked was Sammy Davis, Jr., who became one of my his good friends. Miles had met Sammy earlier on before he had become so popular, and he had also met Harry Belafonte when he was just a young singer doing gigs in small clubs. He knew each of them before they became household words, and I remember them both coming by the house.

I don't remember too much about Sammy at our house, but there's a story my father told me about the time he visited Sammy Davis in the hospital. Sammy was kind of down because he was so sick. The story goes that he was lying in the hospital room with a big ten-gallon hat on. Miles said, "Hey, Sammy, you sure look funny with that small body and that big-assed hat." It totally cracked Sammy up.

I do remember that one day we kids visited Harry Belafonte's house on West End Avenue. It was just up the block from us. It was me, Squeaky, and Cheryl. Frances—my father's wife at the time—was good friends with Belafonte's wife. We had dinner there. Even though we were just kids, Harry was gracious enough to have us all over as special guests.

My father was privy to a lot of celebrities—Black and White—who admired him. They were always dropping by. Sidney Poitier, Redd Foxx, Bill Cosby, Diahann Carroll, Gil Evans, and Harry Belafonte are only some of the names I can recall.

I remember one night Sidney Poitier telling me, "A good physical appearance and being physically together is what Hollywood wants." He said this because at the time I was training to be a boxer, so he was trying to encourage me to stay in good shape.

Another performer that Miles especially loved was Louis Armstrong. Any trumpet player that I've ever talked to also loved Satchmo. He was rightly called the "Father of Jazz."

He became famous because he had his own style, which my father loved. I don't think they ever became friends, but they did meet and talk and everything. Despite all his fame, Louis Armstrong was just a regular guy, as far as I know.

I remember Miles once saying that even his mother loved Louis Armstrong, and that was quite a statement coming from a woman who didn't even want her son to get into the music business.

I was always impressed by the celebrities my father knew. I even once talked to Muhammad Ali on the phone. My father and Muhammed were talking about a Sonny Liston fight. Miles knew I was a fan of Muhammed's. So my father said, "Hey, by the way, my son's over here. Say hello to him. He's a fan of yours." It was just small talk. He said hello to me. Redd Foxx came by one night and signed an autograph for me, telling me that I came from "good stock," and I'll always remember meeting Kareem Abdul-Jabbar and Sugar Ray Robinson. I didn't talk to either of them except to say hi, but my mouth hung open at seeing these sports heroes just sitting around the house. I recall that Sugar Ray not only came over to our house a couple of times, but we also went to his house in Queens. My father and him were buddies. They both appreciated each other as leaders in their professions.

A lot of people came by that house to see Miles and greet him, and I was thrilled by all of this and very respectful to all of those people. But I didn't have all that much awe of them because I knew my father was famous too. To me, they were no more famous in my eyes than my father was.

Billie Holiday Was Really Something Special

Miles and Billie Holiday had a mutual admiration society going between them. I remember when I was a little kid about five or six years old and my father used to take me over to her house in Jamaica, Queens. He'd take a bicycle and put me on the back. In those days that's how we used to get around.

Billie loved me. I still remember how she'd sit me on her lap and run her hands through my hair and tell my father how cute I was and this and that.

She'd say to Miles, "Don't take him. You go, but let him stay here. I'll take care of him." Billie never had any children—maybe because her body was too ravaged with drugs—but she was a nice warm-hearted lady who really loved children.

She and my father never became lovers, but always remained good friends. She was a decade older than him, but really liked Miles's style of music. He was a struggling young musician at the time and I guess she saw something in him. Anything that Billie could do to promote Miles, she'd do it.

I remember me and my father once watching Diana Ross in that movie *Lady Sings the Blues*, which was all about Billie Holiday's life. We also watched *Bird*, the movie Clint Eastwood made about Charlie Parker.

Miles didn't like the way both movies focused on the drugs. He thought that this was pure sensationalism and the kind of bullshit that Hollywood was looking for.

It just saddened my father to watch those movies because he loved both those people and didn't like the way they were portrayed. I can still recall how sad my father was about Billie Holiday dying. A couple of years after she had died her name happened to come up, and my father turned to me and said, "What a waste."

Miles Wasn't a Celebrity Hound

Even though he knew so many famous people, my father was basically a private type of person. You wouldn't find him hanging out around town with celebrities, although they all loved and respected him. He was kind of shy despite all his fame and didn't know what to say to them at public social gatherings.

That was one big reason for his reclusiveness: There were always report-ers at these affairs and anything he had to say—even if it came from his heart—was always interpreted the wrong way. At home, though, in pri-vate conversations it was different. When I was there and some celebrity dropped by, my father had lots to talk about.

When some celebrity he knew was sick or in the hospital, my father would always make that phone call to show his concern, and they'd do the same when he was sick. But Miles rarely went to visit anyone in the hospi-tal because he didn't like those places.

I remember that the celebrity my father most liked being with was the comedian Redd Foxx. They roomed together for a while and were both from St. Louis. Miles said he couldn't sleep half the time because Redd was so funny telling jokes that he'd be up laughing all night.

Rather than running around town and hanging with celebrities, Miles preferred to sit home in front of the TV and drink Heinekens. He enjoyed his isolation, and if there wasn't anybody special in the city performing that night—like Ahmad Jamal, Clark Terry, Jimi Hendrix, or Duke Elling-ton—he wouldn't bother to go out.

Coming up with Charlie Parker he felt that he had heard and seen every-thing. He appreciated all artists, but there were only certain musicians that he loved enough to leave the house and go hear them play. And although my father was not interested in going out to social events of any kind, if his wife or one of his girlfriends wanted to do so he'd accommodate them.

CHAPTER FOURTEEN

So What!
(Kind of Blue, Columbia, 1959)

Miles Didn't Hide from His Audiences

THERE'S A POPULAR MISCONCEPTION that Miles turned his back on his audiences when he performed because he scorned them. That's only partially true. My father often did turn his back on his audience while on-stage, but only because he liked to face the band and direct them.

Of course if you're sitting out there in the audience, your first thought is, "Oh, he's a disrespectful guy." But Miles appreciated his audiences and never felt any disrespect towards them.

Also, a lot of times facing the audience you can get negative feedback or you can be thrown off track. It can cause you to break your concentration. My father was so intent on what he was playing-trying to get that perfect sound-he did not want that to happen. That's another reason why he turned his back to his audiences. But mainly Miles wanted to face the band and direct them.

My mother's version as to why Miles did that is that he was a shy person. He wasn't an athlete-he was slightly built-and maybe that made him feel a little sensitive about his looks. That was his personality.

My father also liked to move a lot around the stage. Miles didn't like the idea of standing up before a microphone and remaining in one spot, so later on in his career he had this electronics engineer in the Netherlands design this wireless system where he could be miked and walk around and play.

Opera singers make use of those wireless mikes today, but I think he was the first or one of the first jazz musicians to have one designed so that he could strap it onto his horn.

My father would always step out of the way when somebody from the band was doing a solo. He didn't want to steal attention from his band members. I remember him once saying, "Never try to play under anybody."

He would also say, "Give the music what it's due but don't play less than anybody." Miles believed in playing what you had to say and then stepping out of the way. Another one of his sayings was, "You gotta complement the music."

When Miles got older, he'd play in a more relaxed position, like pointing his horn to the floor. I guess that was because he could breathe better that way and also because he had had a hip operation.

He was having a hard time standing up straight anymore and playing, because his hip bothered him. But he wasn't sitting down either. A lot of the other players performed sitting down when they got older. But my father always stood up, although he sometimes tended to bend down to the floor.

Miles Tries Telling Some Jokes

My father's road manager once told me something that made me laugh. He said that during one of his tours, Miles decided to try his humor out on his audience—"You know, your father is really funny." It must've been a really rare moment seeing my father standing onstage before playing and telling some jokes. Miles must've been feeling real good about something. It really must've been a wild moment; I wish I had been there to see it.

Talking to the audience when he was onstage was not his usual custom. In fact, when my father was performing he never talked at all. Miles never announced any songs or stuff like that. He'd talk to the band, maybe, but that was about it. Birks was the one who was the clown onstage. That's why they nicknamed him "Dizzy" Gillespie.

Performing with Singers Wasn't His Thing

Miles would listen to singers when he played with them-especially when playing ballads because you have to know the words to a song to play it right and put the right expression on the notes, like "My Funny Valentine."

But as far as I can recall he preferred playing his horn onstage by himself.

Miles would listen to Billie Holiday, Betty Carter, Dinah Washington, Sarah Vaughan, and some South American singers, and even did a couple of records with singers. But for him the horn was always the lead singer and he preferred to keep it that way.

He Was Always Retiring

My father went into his so-called "retirements" on impulse. Other than his health, these hiatuses would depend on his mood and other reasons. Whatever the reason, Miles felt at these moments that he couldn't give his all, one hundred and ten percent, because the horn is a very difficult instrument to play.

Miles was a very eccentric person. If his mood wasn't right, or he felt his mouthpiece wasn't right, or he didn't think he was getting the right kind of money, or something else was wrong, he would put himself in the can for a while. He retired more than a few times, but health was the basic reason why he'd go into one of these retirements.

CHAPTER FIFTEEN

Bitches Brew

(*Columbia, 1969*)

Miles's Women

MY FATHER WAS CLOSE TO A LOT OF WOMEN who went in and out of his life over the years. Some were friends, like Lena Horne, Ava Gardner, and Lana Turner. Others were lovers, like Juliette Greco, an actress who fell in love with my father when he first went over to France in 1949 as part of a tour. My father claimed he was really in love with her, and the story goes that she was deeply in love with him too. But he had to go back to the United States. They tried to keep it together long distance; it just didn't work out.

As much as Miles might have loved her, I don't think he could live anywhere but New York City. He didn't want to move even though he cared about a woman.

Malibu was an exception to the rule. I mean, who wouldn't want to live on the beach for a while? But wherever he was, Miles was always in a New York state of mind—even when he was a thousand miles away from his favorite city.

Wearing His Wives Out

Miles was briefly married to Frances Taylor, who was a dancer; Betty Mabry Davis, a singer; and actress Cicely Tyson. Miles had one last son—Erin—by Marguerite Eskridge. I'm not sure whether she and Miles were ever legally married.

I remember Miles's bringing Erin over to the house when he was no more than five. Miles liked dressing his children up. I remember how Miles used to dress me up in knickers.

I realize now that Miles was trying to create a bond between us. When I last saw Erin at Miles's introduction into the Rock & Roll Hall of Fame in 2006, he embraced me. I have no ill will toward Erin. He is a Davis— my half-brother. I think he knows my heart, and he knows that I loved Miles.

My father would fall in love too easily, being a very passionate kind of person, and before you knew it there was a wedding. He would go on a quick honeymoon, buy his new wife some gifts, and make her happy for a while. They'd live together as long as they could, but then his wife would inevitably split because she couldn't take him anymore.

That's because Miles was so changeable. You'd have to be a special type of woman to stay with a man like that. He could turn into a Mr. Hyde at any moment, and so he'd would wear them out.

Miles was so moody, he was liable to do anything. And if you were his lady you'd feel all that pressure. It was very hard for any woman to stay with a man like that for a long period of time.

You could never pinpoint him. My father would never do the same thing every day. Just when you thought you saw a pattern in his behavior he'd jump up and do something completely different and leave you totally off guard. He just wasn't predictable.

Miles wasn't the kind of man who'd come home every day to have tea. Instead, he might decide not to come home at all or to have tea at the Tavern on the Green.

Or he might decide to have tea at his girlfriend's house, if he happened to have one at the time that his wife didn't even know about. But it was never the same old routine. My father simply was not cut out for that.

Maybe this kind of moody, changeable behavior of his was needed to inspire him in some way and make him feel alive. Maybe he'd get onstage feeling good that he not only had a wife, but a girlfriend too—who knows?

When it came to girlfriends, there was never any shortage. Miles had a lot of opportunities to have all these women with all the groupies that used to chase him around. I'm pretty sure that he always had something going on the side. One woman couldn't fill all his needs. Just ask my mother.

No Marriage Ever Lasted

I always hoped that one of these women who he married would be the one to really help him, and that they could get along for more than just a brief period of time.

I wanted my father to have a good future with each of his marriages, to do positive things with his new wife and for them to strengthen each other. But there was always some kind of demon that came out of him and got between him and his woman.

It was always because of his high expectations that no woman was ever good enough for him, and also because of his changeability, that none of his marriages ever lasted.

Once a woman in his life began complaining about his behavior, it was all over. Miles would get rid of them. There'd be an argument or maybe something worse physically, and they'd have to separate and then part from each other.

Frances Taylor

One of his wives was Frances Taylor, a talented ballet dancer from Chicago who danced with Katharine Dunham in New York. Frances also appeared on Broadway; she was a featured dancer in *West Side Story*. She was a beautiful Black lady, and my father fell in love with her immediately.

Miles married her and soon afterwards began remodeling the townhouse on West 77th Street into a duplex for them. She had her seven-year-old son living with her at the time. So we had a full house there with me, my oldest sister, Cheryl, and my younger brother Squeaky.

I don't know why they split up, but I do know that by then my father had become misogynistic. I guess Miles wanted her to do too many off-the-wall things and I don't think she went for it. She wasn't in that frame of mind because she wasn't down with the drugs.

Miles's mind, though, was racing. He had become schizophrenic and delusional, and it was just too much for her to handle. So Frances divorced him and moved out—another one of his failed marriages.

I remember that relatively speaking she treated me nicely. At first she was possessive of my father and would lay down a lot of rules and regulations for my father and me. I didn't like that.

Also, at that time I was still feeling very attached to my mother, and a protest attitude towards Miles marrying someone else showed up in me a little bit. But not to the point where I'd argue with her or anything like that.

I know that my father really loved her, but with Miles there was always another woman, and the next one was Cicely Tyson. Then, after Cicely split on him—probably for the same reasons that Frances did—there was Jo Gelbard. She was with him at the time in California when Miles was sick and close to dying.

Miles's Last Girlfriend

Jo was an accomplished sculptor and painter who he met in New York City. He was 58 and married to Cicely. Jo was 34 and lived in the same building as Miles.

Miles had taken up art, and she visited his apartment and helped him with his painting. From collaborating on Miles's art, things progressed. Jo really tried to take good care of my father and encouraged him to move out to California for a change of scenery. Out there, she gave him vitamins and even took him swimming to try and improve his health.

Jo was my father's last girlfriend. They had known each other for seven years. She was the one who called me and told me to come right away to the hospital in California (after my own so-called sister decided not to tell me exactly how serious his situation was).

She said, "Gregory, he talks about you all the time, and I think you should really be here. He's really sick this time. Tell your family to send you a ticket."

Of course my family refused to do so (and a day later he was dead). When Miles took sick, Vernon, Dorothy, and Cheryl were there, I'm told. I also remember Jo telling me, "I try to sleep in the room when they allow me to." That's how much the faamily cared for him.

I don't know if they paid for their own tickets, but Trumpet Productions usually paid for the family's airfare. When Jo called, I asked her if arrangements could be made for me to see my father. Nothing happened. When the will was probated, Jo was deposed. My attorney asked her whether Miles ever said anything about there being ill (will) between us. She said no. Funny, seven years together, and Miles never said a word about the so-called rift we had.

Jo seemed real nice over the phone. All I know is that she did not testify in my favor as far as probating the will was concerned.

Miles Wanted More Than Just Sex

I remember when I was living with him, I used to have a lot of girlfriends. Some of them would come over and clean my little apartment and cook me something to eat. My father would say to me, "Where'd you get her from?"

Then she'd come down and clean his apartment and he was kind of amazed. The girls he had would never do that. It might damage their fingernails or something. They'd just come and go like revolving doors.

I think Miles respected a woman who would take his clothes to the laundry, clean the house, and cook him something besides just giving him some sex or be with him only to do drugs.

Deep in his heart, Miles Davis was really an old-fashioned guy who wanted more than just sex. Despite being the genius that he was, everyday mundane things were part of his life, too, and he thought it was great that a woman would do these kinds of things for him. He grew up in a traditional house where women cooked the food and took care of the cleaning and the children, and he wanted some of that in his life—not just women who were hangers-on. He was impressed by a woman who could show concern about something other than what night spots they were going to hit that evening. It made him feel that this woman really cared about him and that maybe he should think more seriously about her.

I Wasn't Mad That Miles Left My Mother

People sometimes ask me if I was mad at my father for having left my mother, Irene Cawthon Davis, whom he had married in 1942. Maybe in the beginning I was. Maybe I thought that he had betrayed her. It was always in my head, as to why they had to separate.

Divorce or separation always affects children, but it didn't affect me to the point where I couldn't finish my schoolwork or anything like that—especially because both Miles and my mother were always available to me. From time to time, though, I thought about what had happened between the two of them. It taught me that life is bittersweet, that life is not perfect.

It would've been much harder if Miles had said, "I don't want to see none of those kids." But he didn't. He was always in our lives. Never once did either my father or mother say, "I hate those kids and I don't want to be around them, so you take them," or that kind of thing. It was never like that.

So despite their being apart there was some kind of psychological equilibrium that didn't make things too hard for me or the other siblings. I began to see that Miles was a father to me whether or not he was separated from my mother.

It's true that my mother went through some financial difficulties raising us because of that separation, although we didn't spend one day on welfare. Still, Miles never stopped supporting her.

My Mother Wasn't Upset Either

All this running around and marrying different women didn't bother my mother much, as far as I could tell. She knew Miles from the time they were high school sweethearts and was glad that she knew him when he had his purity, before his personality was twisted by his inability to handle success or drugs.

He did not know how to handle his gift of genius. He was insecure—a fish out of water—and didn't have the emotional maturity or willpower to get out of the Miles Davis persona and into his normal self.

But my mother would always remember my father as the shy guy he was back then—a person who loved clothes like she did—and how they'd always go to the stores looking at the latest fashions. My mother preferred to remember things like that—the movies they went to on dates and the chocolates he used to buy her.

In fact, my mother knew Miles's personality so well that she could almost predict what was going to happen next when he got involved with another woman. Still, she was more concerned with her own life and raising us kids than getting jealous or upset over my father's erratic lifestyle.

She wanted the best for us, the best clothes on our backs and enough money for us to live in the best neighborhoods, so she didn't have time to be sitting around feeling bitter about her separation from my father.

They weren't hostile to each other. They always spoke on the phone. It was just that they grew apart. They never talked to me personally about any of this, but I just used to watch their behavior.

I think if there was any bitterness between them, It was more on my father's part than my mother's, because she had other men after they were separated. My mother got married, had another child—my youngest sister, Raymelle—and I think Miles was always jealous about that.

Miles would always leave her completely out of things, even when he was buying us Christmas gifts or something like that. How do you think that would make a child feel? But despite such treatment I know that she always cared for Miles and the rest of us.

I think that by treating Raymelle in that coolish manner, Miles believed he was somehow getting even with my mother. It was the same with me and Little Miles later on in years. He'd think that by doing some things that would hurt us he'd be hurting her.

As petty as it sounds, that's how my father could be in his deluded thoughts towards the end of his life.

CHAPTER SIXTEEN

A Tribute to Jack Johnson
(*Soundtrack, Columbia, 1970*)

Miles's Obsession with Sports

THINK MY FATHER'S BIG INTEREST in boxing came from my grandfather, who always enjoyed sports. So my father grew up loving boxing. The trumpet being a rather physical instrument, you had to be in good shape to play it. Working out in the boxing ring was his way to stay in shape to play his horn.

When you look at a sports hero in action, it's like he's an artist himself. And my father appreciated seeing that. He especially liked a fighter named Johnny Bratton who could fight with either hand. He could do everything with his left hand that he could do with his right, although his hands were always fragile and he would break them. But he was a sensation to watch, and my father used to love to go to the fights to see him. He also admired Sugar Ray Robinson and Joe Louis. Jack Johnson was another athlete that my father really appreciated.

Miles loved sports in general, not just boxing. He'd sit in front of that TV of his and would always be watching baseball, basketball, and films of classic boxing matches.

My father even had films of fights with Sugar Ray Robinson, Johnny Bratton, Jack Dempsey, Gene Tunney, and Jack Johnson. He knew these guys who used to promote fights at the Garden, and they'd give him these films. Miles would always run them for me. We'd sit down together along with my brother and watch them.

Jack Johnson

Jack Johnson was a fighter my father really admired. He came along and became a hero at a time when the Black man wasn't supposed to do that sort of thing.

Johnson became the first Black boxing champion. All of his wives were White. He played bass and drove fast sports cars. Miles really liked that kind of independent thinking. The fighter reminded him of himself. He was an independent thinker too, and he was never content with just being a Negro and staying in his place.

Jack Johnson never had that kind of slave attitude. He said, "I'm gonna be free. I'm gonna be a man and I'm gonna spend my money any way I like and enjoy my life." That was Miles, too. He and my father were almost the same kind of people.

Boxing and Me

My father was always taking me to boxing matches and baseball games. He also encouraged me to box, and I did so. I used to box in amateur fights at clubs like the Catholic Youth Organization in New York City, and I won every fight I ever had. When I went into the service overseas, I won two championships. I weighed 139 at the time and I was in the light welterweight division.

As a matter of fact, my godfather, Clark Terry, has one of my trophies that I presented to him along with the Miles Davis mute and horn bag to put in Clark's archives at William Patterson University. Clark had a long-standing relationship with the student band there and asked me for some mementos from my father's career.

Whenever I asked Miles to come watch me fight in the city, he'd kiddingly put his hands over his face like, "Oh, no, I don't want to see you get hurt."

He knew I was a good fighter, but I think he just didn't want to see his son being knocked around. So instead of coming himself, he'd ask his drummer, Philly Joe Jones, to escort me. Miles would tell him, "Take him there, he's got a match tonight."

When I came out of the service with an honorable discharge, Miles looked at me and said, "You've done something for your country, now do something for yourself."

He meant that I should not only keep myself in top-notch physical shape, but I should also get a muscle in my brain and go to school. I thought so too. I knew what I could do with my body, but what could I do with my mind?

Miles was tough on me when it came to my training, and he'd make sure that I kept to my regimen. We were living in his building on West 77th Street and I'd get up every other day around six o'clock in the morning and run around the Central Park reservoir to do my little workout.

Then I'd come home, have some tea, get my books, and go to class— I was in junior high school then. Later in the afternoon, after school, I'd go to Harry Wylie's gym on 135th Street. I had my own trainer there that my father hired.

Harry was connected with Sugar Ray Robinson, who Miles admired a lot. A lot of well-known fighters used to train there, like Muhammad Ali and Doug Jones. So that was my routine. I'd usually get home by six o'clock, study for school, and fall asleep dead tired.

I remember that sometimes Miles would surprise me and punch me in the stomach when I had drunk too much or something. It would be play punching, but he still hit you hard and it hurt. My father would laugh and say, "Not in shape, huh? Look at you stumbling."

I'd say "Yeah" and not become angry, because I knew my father was being good-intentioned when he did that. He didn't want me to drink too much and get out of shape.

Miles would do that punching thing to a lot of people, and they didn't like it because they didn't know where he was coming from when he did that, whether he was serious or not.

He Worked Out at the Gym

My father wasn't in any boxing matches like I was, but he'd also go to the gym to work out and keep himself in shape. When I was a kid and we lived for a while in Chicago, me and my father used to go to Johnny Coulon's gym. He was a White guy who had won a bantamweight championship way back in 1914. Coulon and his wife ran the gym and he was a very nice guy.

Miles would punch bags, work up a sweat skipping rope, work out in the ring, beat the speed bag—things to build up his sweat and get those impurities out. My father realized the importance of exercise for his breathing when he was playing the horn, and then afterwards he would always get a rubdown.

Miles Could Knock You Out

My father could defend himself pretty well, but he'd have to have an equalizer like a knife or a gun or a piece of wood or something if the guy he was facing was a big dude, because Miles was really a small-statured guy.

Despite his size, if my father got the jump on you, you'd be knocked right out even if you were bigger than him. He really could hit. If you messed around with him and let him get the jump on you, he would knock you out. However, without that element of surprise, I think a big guy could've squashed him.

Some books say that my father was abusive to men as well as women. But when it came to men, he'd only be playing around with them. That wasn't the case with women in his life.

With his close male friends, Miles would pretend that he was angry with something they said or did. He'd say, "You old White muthafucka, you." And the guy would say, "Miles, I'm gonna kick your ass," or something like that.

My father would grin because he was not serious in the first place. He just wanted to get a reaction. He said it out of friendship because he was never a racist. He was just making a joke out of things. Then he would put his arm around the guy and they'd go have a drink.

But sometimes he wasn't just fooling around.

I remember when I was acting as his bodyguard that we were in this joint and my father got into an argument with some guy. They ended up calling each other names, and the guy wanted to beat him up.

This was right after my father had a joint operation and this dude wanted to push him around even though I was right there with him. I couldn't let that happen, so I knocked the guy out. Then the guy ended up apologizing to my father.

That's one of the instances of what I mean when I say that my father would take you out on a limb and leave you there. I mean, why was he cursing at this dude in the first place when I was the only one there to defend him? I was the one that had to go out on a limb to protect him. I had to stand between him and the guy to make sure he didn't hurt my father.

Let me tell you one thing, though, Miles was no coward. He'd always let you know exactly what was on his mind whether or not you liked it. Sometimes he couldn't back up his words, and he'd almost get his ass kicked.

There were a lot of times when Miles opened his mouth and I had to step in tostop that from happening.

He Respected People Who Stood Up for Themselves

Miles always respected a man with strong character or a strong personality. He thought Henry Kissinger was not only tough but also smart. My father also respected Elijah Muhammad—not for hating White people, but for trying to give some structure to the Black community.

Elijah Muhammad was always talking about cleaning your house up, respecting your woman, respecting yourself, and getting your own businesses started. While Miles wasn't able to follow some of that advice himself, he nonetheless respected Muhammad for speaking out about those things.

Although he fell short of it, my father respected a man who could clean himself up, straighten out his life, and take care of his family because my grandfather was that kind of man and my ancestors were those kinds of people.

The Davises all took charge of their families and stood up and faced the world like men. That's why I feel that my ancestors are rolling over in their graves because of Miles not taking charge and making sure all his family were provided for after he died. I just know that our ancestors would not like his behavior one bit.

My Father Knocks Out His Lawyer

One time Miles knocked out Harold Lovette from the Lovette-Wright law firm. Lovette was his first lawyer and helped Miles get the settlement after he was attacked by the cop outside of Birdland.

Harold was a smart guy and another fine dresser, although he was thin and not well built. He worked for my father for a long time. But he drank too much, and one night he obviously said the wrong thing to Miles. So my father punched him out.

When he got up he said, "Miles, did you hit me?"

My father grinned and said, "No."

CHAPTER SEVENTEEN

Miles, Miles, Miles

(Sony, 1981)

Miles's Favorite and Private Things

THERE WERE A LOT OF THINGS BESIDES MUSIC, DRUGS, AND WOMEN that my father loved—from clothes and expensive cars to racehorses—and things that he didn't love, like inequality, bigots, and music critics. I want to take a few moments here to tell you about some of his favorites.

Clothes Were One of His Favorite Things

My father used to love buying shoes. He loved Italian shoes and French shoes. In fact, if Miles found a pair of shoes that he liked, he'd buy two pairs of them. He'd smile and say to me, "Now I got a reserve pair."

Miles also loved leather, but he couldn't work in leather because he sweated too much. My father really loved fine clothes and had all his suits custommade. Sometimes he'd even create fashion trends by wearing this or that.

I credit my father for being the one to make a dark-skinned Black man seem fashionable and in vogue. That's because society—and many African-Americans themselves—always looked at the lighter-skinned Blacks as the ones who epitomized their race.

But my father, with his dark skin and flair for fashion, helped to change that image. I remember that he was always together with his clothes and with his sharp appearance, making Black look beautiful.

Miles was such an articulate dresser that he was even once featured in *Esquire* magazine as one of the best-dressed people—Black or White. He knew what he liked and would only buy the best.

My father loved the way Fred Astaire danced and also the way he dressed. He also liked the way Harry James, Cary Grant, the Duke of Windsor, and

Dexter Gordon dressed. So Miles would always wear expensive Italian and French suits and shoes.

Miles would always take me shopping with him. We'd go to places like Saks Fifth Avenue and he'd buy me expensive clothes too. A love for clothes must have run in the family, because even when I was staying with my father and mother in Brooklyn before they split, she would take my shirts to the Chinese laundry and make sure they were pressed. And she also placed an emphasis on fashion.

This wasn't a time when everyone was wearing jeans like they are today. You'd go to school wearing a white shirt and a tie. One time the Chinese laundry lost one of my shirts and I still remember how furious my mother was.

Both my parents made sure I was well dressed. One time they even dressed me in knickers and all the dummies in the neighborhood laughed at me. No one had ever seen anything like it, but Miles knew that in London wearing knickers was a sign of class.

I also wore silk scarves and blazers, and that also looked strange to all the knuckleheads in the neighborhood. They had no idea about classy clothes, but my mother and father sure did.

It was my mother and father who taught me how to dress and all about clothes, and it was Miles's father and mother who had taught him the same thing. They were always aware of style and fabric and who made the best suits and how to get the best value for your money.

I liked to dress that way because I thought it was cool and exciting. Today, I still appreciate how Miles and my mother gave me a taste for fine clothes and fine cars and all the other finer things in life. That's what you want your parents to expose you to—not drugs.

Miles's Passion for Expensive Cars

When my father was living on 57th Street, he had a 190 SL Mercedes parked outside the building even though he didn't have much money back then.

Later on, when he could afford to buy his building on 77th Street, and when he lived in Malibu, Miles owned a series of Ferraris including a Ferrari Dino. He was really into Ferraris and other classic cars like Mercedes and Jaguars. My father had a passion for expensive cars and had fine taste in just about everything else.

I guess his taste in fine cars also came from my grandfather. Back home, my grandfather always drove a Cadillac. I recall that on one of my grandfather's birthdays, Miles sent him one of those expensive, classic Jaguars—the kind with all the interior wood paneling.

My father used to drive me around a lot in New York, and I thought he could drive well except for those times that he was inebriated and didn't give a damn about anything, including his own life.

I remember one night we were speeding down 72nd Street to where his garage was, and he was high as can be. I had to tell him, "Hey, wait a minute now, I'm in this car too. What are you doing? Slow down." Miles was in a different frame of mind and trying to drive. He looked at me like he was coming out of a spell and then kind of got it together and slowed down.

Driving a Car at Age 12

I remember that one day my father drove us to Philadelphia in this beautiful red Ferrari because he had a gig there. We stayed at a little motel somewhere in the city.

A day or two later, he wanted to go back to New York City because his former girlfriend, Beverly Garland, was getting married to Norman Mailer. Mailer had somehow managed to steal her away from him. Miles was kind of melancholy about it and wanted to say goodbye to her.

So we drove to the Philadelphia train station and my father turns to me and says, "Here's the keys. You drive it back to the motel." The problem was that I was only 12 years old and didn't know how to drive. That didn't seem to bother Miles one bit.

So I drove that Ferrari. I was missing gears and grinding gears and stuff, and I think the police looked over at me and said, "No, Bill, this can't be it. There can't be a Black kid driving a Ferrari. We're dreaming." So the police never stopped me. That's just another example of how Miles could leave you out on a limb.

When he got back the next day, his car was safely back in the motel parking lot and the keys were on the table in the room. He had a big smile on his face and he was real happy about that, but we never discussed the subject of him letting me drive at age 12.

Miles Loved to Cook

My father loved French and Southern cooking—especially French-style bouillabaisse dishes. He also loved to barbecue outside and make pork ribs and that kind of stuff. Later on, when he learned more about nutrition, he learned not to eat so much of that pork.

Miles liked to toss stuff together and thought he was a chef because he had been over to France and learned how to cook some French-style dishes. But I must admit that he really did cook those bouillabaisse dishes well.

Another of his favorite foods was rice and black beans with Italian bread. Miles also liked to make salads with shrimp and squid added to it. Even when he had a new girlfriend my father would do the cooking because they usually weren't good at it. They were just good lookers, not good cookers, and my father would have to show them what to do.

I remember as youngsters when we were over at his 77th Street place, that Miles would always do some of the cooking along with Frances. As far as I can recall, we hardly ever ate out.

Sitting at the dinner table, I remember my father always asking us kids how our schoolwork was, did we do our homework, and how I was doing at the gym. It was mostly small talk or mundane things, like for us to make sure the house was kept neat and that we take showers and keep our bodies clean. Miles was always grooming himself and teaching us to do the same.

My father would also remind us that he spent a lot of money on that house and it was our job to do the chores or, at least, to keep our rooms clean and make sure the dining room was always washed and waxed because his friends were always dropping by.

When Frances Taylor became his wife and moved in, Miles's much more pleasant side would emerge at the dinner table. I remember that he was very loving and treated Frances like a kitten. My father would even hand-feed her and they'd act like they were newlyweds. It was a pleasure to watch!

Taking a Lot of Sleeping Pills

My father was addicted to sleeping pills. He was so active and put so much energy into his work that he had to take them to calm down at night.

They were very strong pills and I knew that if he took enough of them that he could kill himself. Hollywood stars have the same kind of stuff and you always read in the papers how so-and-so overdosed on them. These stars are a lot like my father was—highly emotional, highly competitive, and tense—so that's why I worried about him.

Miles often had a hard time sleeping, so he was always taking these pills. He was too revved up, just like a racehorse. My father had pill boxes filled with sleeping pills in the medicine cabinet, and he was always going to the pharmacy to pick up another prescription. It was one yet one more thing that Miles was hooked on.

He Enjoyed Painting

Even when they were kids, Miles and his brother Vernon liked art and did some painting. But it was only later on in life that my father took a real interest in it.

Miles felt that he had accomplished some of his musical goals, so he explored art for a while and began to paint abstracts.

He also had a couple of girlfriends who encouraged him to paint, among them Jo Gelbard. Miles also had a couple of male painter friends who pushed him into it.

So he started experimenting and putting stuff on canvas. I didn't really think he would take it as far as he did, but when I saw the results of his work I was really impressed.

You really have to study art to be a true painter, so I call what my father did "doodling around." He wasn't a great painter or anything like that, he was just giving vent to his creative expression.

Miles would always know more about music, but he enjoyed doing art. Nowadays, however, people take those "doodles" quite seriously and his work is worth a piece of money.

Eastwood and Brando

Another one of my father's favorite things was watching Clint Eastwood movies, especially *The Eiger Sanction*. He also loved Marlon Brando movies until one day he somehow found out that Brando had hit on Frances. Brando always liked exotic types of women, and Frances had those looks.

On TV, besides watching anything that had to do with sports, from boxing to car racing, Miles enjoyed soap operas. He used to laugh and say, "Look, rich White people have more problems than Black people."

Gangster movies were also among his favorites, especially those classic old ones with James Cagney and Humphrey Bogart. He liked to see how they would dress and how they would act. My father just loved that movie *The Public Enemy*, where James Cagney squashes this grapefruit into Mae Clarke's face.

Miles loved to read too. When I was older and just hanging out with him at 77th Street, Miles mostly would sit on the couch and read magazines and books of all kinds—he went through them very quickly. If he wasn't reading, then my father would lie around the house and we'd watch TV, mostly boxing films.

His Feud with Max Roach

Someone who got on his "muthafucka" list and wasn't among his favorites was the famous drummer Max Roach, who played with Charlie Parker's band and was in Miles's band. Roach was the drummer on *Birth of the Cool*. Max came along the same time my father did, and for a long time they were good friends.

Miles and Max had a serious falling out over a 1961 Miles Davis/Gil Evans concert in which Max staged a sit-down protest against the African Relief Foundation. But I think they had their real falling out over Max's girlfriend, Abbey Lincoln, the jazz singer. If I remember the story right, Max thought Miles was dating Abbey on the sly.

That resulted in a big argument between the two of them, so from good friends they became bitter enemies. Later on, though, they reconciled because they both respected each other.

Speaking Out for Equality

Standing on a bandstand to proclaim his political or social views was not Miles's style. He was not a Jane Fonda or somebody like that. He preferred a quieter approach to expressing how he felt about things.

Miles used his acclaim to quietly speak out for equality for Black people—and for people of all colors who were oppressed or discriminated against—but only if he was asked for his opinion. Then my father certainly wasn't afraid to speak up and tell it like it is about prejudice, institutionalized and personal, in this country or anywhere else.

As I said before, my father was not a racist. If you got to know him and became his friend he didn't care what color you were. And he wasn't an elitist either. Miles didn't like to see or read about poverty or hear about any kind of inequities among people.

Once, when he traveled to Mexico, he was appalled by the poverty he saw there. Miles would reach into his pocket and throw out loose change to the kids from the train he was riding on.

Like all great artists, Miles had a tremendous following, so everything from how he dressed to what he played and said had great influence on his thousands of fans. He had become an "institution" in his own right.

Still, he refrained from being a political activist. Privately, however, he would express his feelings and talk about how he supported Martin Luther King. In fact, Miles once mentioned to me that Coretta Scott King was some kind of distant cousin.

Even today, years after his death, Miles remains an institution, one of his kind like James Dean. Walking around New York City, I think I see just as many Miles Davis posters in windows of stores as I do of Dean or Marilyn Monroe, and his music still continues to sell very well.

Desmond Tutu Was One of His Favorites

Because of his distaste for inequality, Miles really appreciated Desmond Tutu and what he was doing to fight racism in Africa. My father even did an album called *Tutu*; it was his first album on the Warner Bros. label after he had switched from Columbia, and it won him a Grammy in 1987.

One of the reasons my father hated bigotry in any form is that he was sometimes exposed to it as a young man back in St. Louis, and also because of that incident outside Birdland.

I remember one time how pissed off he got when he read that in California all the way up to the 1940s a Black musician couldn't work with a White musician. "Can you imagine that?," he said to me.

Miles Didn't Like Music Critics

Also on his un-favorites list were music critics. Sure, if it was positive criticism—if it had something good to say about his music—Miles loved it, but otherwise he couldn't stand critics. He thought that most of the time they were full of crap and didn't know what the hell they were talking about.

Some of these critics used to call him the "Prince of Darkness" because of the enigma he created by turning his back on the audience. He also didn't talk much like a lot of performers did, so he seemed rather mysterious to them.

Miles didn't like that description of himself. Being draped with that title was yet one more reason why my father couldn't stand most music critics or, for that matter, most reporters. To my father, that nickname was pure bullshit—more of a buildup of his mystique, which he didn't think was him. He had a shy personality and that's all there was to his turning his back to the audience. He also wanted to listen to himself and be more attuned to what he and the band were doing with the music—not lose his attention. It was more important for him to play for himself and the other musicians—but, at the same time, not to forget his audience.

He Wasn't Much on Politics

Politics wasn't among his favorite subjects, and my father hardly discussed it with me. I'm not even sure that he ever even voted, although I do know that he was a Democrat. Miles did, however, express an appreciation for affirmative action.

The few times I ever did hear him discussing politics, Miles said that he disliked conservatives because they were against change and change was a cornerstone of his life.

There Wasn't Too Much Miles Feared

I don't recall Miles ever talking about being afraid of death. I don't think he ever thought he was going to die. Even when he was dying, Jo told me how much he struggled against it to the very end.

If my father was afraid of anything, it was that me and his other kids wouldn't succeed in life. Despite all of his erratic and often bizarre behavior toward us, Miles nonetheless wanted us to do the best that we could do in life. That's why he got so upset with me during the period when I was doing a little drugs.

I think aging was also something he was a little fearful of—losing his looks so he could no longer attract young women. I remember how Miles would sometimes look at me and say, "If I had all that hair, I wouldn't wear a hat. Look at you. You got all this hair and you're covering it up." I was younger then and had a lot of hair, while he was getting balder.

He must've forgotten that when I was a young man he bought me a fedora. He said, "You're gettin' to be a man and you should be wearin' this." My father used to like wearing those fedoras.

So he took me to the store and bought me one of those hats. But he'd jokingly tell me, "You gotta watch out how you wear these, Greg, or they'll think you're some kind of gangster."

He Valued Education and Hard Work

Miles did not come from a family that was poor. He came from a family with a hardworking father who appreciated education as a means to uplift himself economically and socially. My grandfather's family had a lot of children, and I think every one of them went to college.

My father appreciated the same values of education and hard work. He really appreciated the fact that in the days when Negroes were blocked from making economic progress, a Black man like his grandfather ended up being one of the wealthiest men in the state.

Miles, however, never felt that he came from a privileged family—just a hardworking one. The lessons of education combined with hard work were instilled in him when he was very young and he never forgot them. It was his hard work combined with his talent which ultimately led to his success.

He Just Wanted to Be Himself

I don't think that becoming famous was a thought that ever entered my father's mind. At least I never heard him talking about that being one of his goals. It just so happened that he *was* great.

My father worked hard with the talent he had and did the best he could. If he turned out great, well, he believed that's just the way it was supposed to be. If he didn't, that's the way it was supposed to be also.

I do think that after a while his ego took over and he did become impressed with his own fame. One thing he didn't like, though, was the kind of fame where the papers were calling him things like the "Prince of Darkness."

I also think that sometimes, when his ego wasn't in control, Miles was a little surprised at the fame he had achieved because he really was a country boy at heart.

You know, often when you become famous and achieve notoriety it shocks and surprises you. You don't even recognize yourself anymore because they've made something different of you.

If there was anything else my father didn't like about all his fame, it was that he had to put on that Miles Davis mask whenever he stepped outside his house. He had to be what the public had created him to be. But Miles just wanted to be himself.

My father had a certain amount of insecurity because society gave him all this notoriety and he didn't feel he was all that they were making him out to be. He simply did all his work out of a love and passion for music.

But the public had turned him into something larger than life, and I think it was hard for him to cope with that. Now he was three personalities instead of just one: Dr. Jekyll, Mr. Hyde, and some kind of superstar.

As far as his musical ability went, my father never had any doubts about that. It didn't mean he had become complacent. Miles was always listening to all different types of music, experimenting with various combinations of sounds and styles, and trying to evolve musically.

He was like some Einstein, always theorizing about how to incorporate different forms of music into his way of playing.

Religion Wasn't His Favorite Thing

Miles really didn't believe in anything but himself. I don't remember him going to church much or anything like that even when I was a kid. My father knew there was a God out there and that if he'd do some of the work then God would do the rest. With my father, it got to the point where he felt he was doing most of the work.

My father's talent was a God-given gift, but it tortured him. It was a burden as well as a gift. Miles was like Beethoven and a lot of these great artists over the centuries who were tortured by their genius.

They were all given special gifts, but they sure paid a high price for it. If Miles had been able to find some way to change his negative energy, I'm sure he would have lived a longer and healthier life.

Because my father didn't show much interest in religion over the years that I lived with him, neither did I. When I was a kid my grandmother and my mother used to take me to church, but I really didn't like it because it seemed to be much ado about nothing. It just took up my time and was really boring.

Then later on in life I started to read books about Islam and became impressed with it. Eventually I converted and became a Muslim. I felt that God created us all and didn't need to pick out one son to save us, as Christianity preached.

Even before that, I was a follower of Elijah Muhammad, but it was for political, not religious, reasons. He had a political program that was actually giving more unity and self-esteem to Black people and I liked that. So did my father.

Christianity never did that. It was a religion forced on us by our slave masters. But Elijah Muhammad emphasized values and morals and encouraged Black people to go to school and pursue career goals.

My father was delighted with the new sense of self-esteem that I was developing as a follower of Elijah Muhammad. Miles, as I've already said, admired strong people and Elijah Muhammad was one of them.

But when Elijah Muhammad started talking about hating White folks, that's when my father lost interest in him. His attitude on this subject made me have second thoughts about my own racial feelings, which until then had been somewhat anti-White. Eventually I grew disillusioned with Muhammad when I heard about money scandals that were affecting his Nation of Islam. Today, my closest friends include people of all faiths and colors, and I'm glad about that.

CHAPTER EIGHTEEN

Someday My Prince Will Come

(*Columbia, 1961*)

Miles Wanted to Raise Horses

MY FATHER HAD HIS SHARE OF DREAMS, and one of them was that someday he'd retire and become a gentleman farmer out in Connecticut or somewhere he could breed thoroughbred horses. One time he told me, "All I ever wanted was a horse farm."

But he never achieved that dream, not because he didn't have enough money to do so—I mean, when Miles died he left over $13 million including stocks and property and whatever (despite what other books have said)—but because he didn't have enough time.

With his recording schedule and all the concerts his record company had him scheduled for, he was always busy. Raising horses would mean that he'd have to stop playing music and spend some time setting the whole thing up, and he just wasn't ready to do that.

Some people told me that my father owned some shares in a racehorse. But what he wanted most was a horse farm. Miles liked the racetrack, but I think his real interest in racehorses came from my grandfather, who loved them. (My grandfather was also big on betting the ponies, and the family always talked about how he loved to play them.)

Gambling, however, was one vice I never heard that my father was into although I know that once in a while he'd place a bet—I think a little bit of my grandfather rubbed off on him."

My grandfather's farm at Millstadt was an old German settlement in Illinois right outside of East St. Louis that had a lot of animals running around on it—especially hogs, which he raised. There was also one horse, which I think he called Bob.

Because Miles admired his grandfather so much, I'm sure that this was the impetus for my father's dream of breeding thoroughbreds.

Getting into the Movies

Miles tried his hand at a lot of things, including acting. He wrote some songs for movies and then even made guest television appearances on *Miami Vice* and *Crime Story*. I didn't like the role he played on *Miami Vice*. He played a pimp who gets killed at the end of the episode. Miles also had a small role in the Bill Murray movie *Scrooged*, in which he played a street musician.

Finding Himself

Besides trying to fulfill his artistic ambitions and his dreams, my father was always searching for himself. I don't think he ever accomplished that on a personal level, but he was comfortable with himself when it came to his musical career.

Miles was able to look back on his accomplishments and smile, because he did what he always wanted to do. He had come a long way from that young and inexperienced horn player in St. Louis. He had made it to the big time.

My father wasn't the kind of man to do something that he didn't enjoy doing. It had to be something that he enjoyed or he just wouldn't do it—he'd go into retirement or take more drugs or something.

But the fact that he was still performing showed that my father liked where he was at. He was able to play what he wanted to play and that made him, at least on a musical level, a satisfied man.

CHAPTER NINETEEN

Seven Steps to Heaven
(Columbia, 1963)

I Find Out Miles Is Dying

IT WAS SOMETIME IN AUGUST OR SEPTEMBER 1991, in the last few days of my father's life, that his girlfriend at the time, Jo Gelbard, called me from California. I was in New York, studying to become a psychotherapist.

Jo said, "Your father talks about you all the time; you really should be here." It was then that I learned that Miles was in St. John's Hospital in Santa Monica, where he was admitted on Labor Day. He'd been vomiting blood and Jo thought he'd gotten pneumonia again—something he suffered from intermittently since he began doing drugs.

When I was living with my father, I had always been taking him back and forth to the hospital because of his drug-induced lifestyle. So I said, "What is it this time?"

Then she filled me in on the seriousness of the situation. Jo also told me that my father had been cheating on his diet. "He'd sit in front of the TV and eat ice cream and cookies," she said.

I knew that, being a diabetic, he just couldn't do that. You had to take your insulin. But Miles always had it his own way, and he was not following that regimen.

I mean, I know some people who have diabetes and have to eat something before they take insulin, but it's certainly not ice cream and cookies. And who knows how much of that junk he ate sitting in front of the television watching boxing or whatever.

Jo kept repeating, "Your father talks about you all the time," and telling me that I needed to be there. "Tell them to send for you. He's really past that line." So I called my sister and my aunt because I wanted to be by his side but couldn't afford a plane ticket.

I had just bought a house for my wife and two little kids and had entered Long Island University, which all cost me a ton of money. I was broke and needed some financial help to make that trip out to California. But they wouldn't help me. So while I really wanted to be there for my father because I knew that he needed me, I was unable to do so.

I'm sure that in his time of need Miles really expected my family and his manager to do the right thing and get me there. I was always the one he could lean on and trust when he was in deep trouble. But they didn't do the right thing. As Jo said in her deposition, Trumpet Productions, one of Miles's companies, usually picked up the tab for the family's airfare—but not for me. I can only conclude that they didn't want me there before my father died.

A few days later Miles had a stroke and the left side of his body was paralyzed. He went into a coma and then he was gone.

My father was sixty-five years old and weighed about 90 pounds when he died. Jo told me that like the fighters he always admired, he kept battling against falling asleep and was pulling all the tubes out of him.

She later also told me that Miles kept repeating, "I don't wanna die. I don't wanna die." But this was one round in life that my father lost. The official cause of death was listed as pneumonia, respiratory failure, and a stroke.

Seeing Him at the Funeral Home

I saw my father for the last time when they brought his body back to New York City, the town he always loved best. To tell you the truth, I didn't really want to see him.

I just wanted to remember him the way he was when he was alive. I wanted to remember the good times we once had together and celebrate his life rather than mourn his death.

I went to the funeral home with my family members. When I was inside I walked up to his casket and tried to lift my father's arm. It felt like a piece of lead because it was so heavy with all that junk—the embalming fluid—they had injected him with.

Those moments are something I still don't like to remember because it was so morbid. My memories of his memorial are a lot better. Wesley Snipes was there and a lot of other celebrities. Mayor David Dinkins and the Reverend Jesse Jackson both gave eulogies for my father.

The memorial was held at St Peter's Lutheran Church in midtown Manhattan. The place was packed. There were relatives and musicians and many of his fans all crushed into the church. I recall sitting there with my children listening to all the guest speakers who spoke of their remembrances of him—people like Wesley Snipes. They were playing "Kind of Blue" in the background and I think the service lasted about two hours.

My two daughters—Ena and Antoinnette—were there, and my son, Khalid. Khalid even got a chance to speak to Wesley Snipes afterwards. I remember that there was a big picture of Miles on the stage.

I was sitting there thinking that I had lost a father that I loved and what the future was going to be without him in my life. I remember also hoping that he had done the right thing in his will because I had children that I wanted to make sure had a good education and I was not a wealthy man. I didn't do much talking to anyone there that day, just a lot of thinking about the years we had spent together—a man who I always respected, and who I always helped when he needed a helping hand.

We buried Miles along with his trumpet in Woodlawn Cemetery in the Bronx. His mausoleum was just adjacent to where his good friend Duke Ellington was buried. Miles had wanted it that way because he really loved Duke and especially appreciated his music.

My father's monument said: "In Memory of Sir Miles Davis, 1926–1991."

My Brother Hated My Father

Little Miles wasn't at the memorial or the funeral because he hated my father. Squeaky blamed Miles for his lot in life. My brother hated Miles so much that he changed his name to Mohammed largely because he didn't want the Davis last name. I talk to my brother today, but I didn't for a while after he allegedly slapped my mother.

My mother had become aware that Squeaky and I had been disinherited and one afternoon she took Little Miles to lunch. While they were eating she told him, "Look, your brother's in this with you, so stick with him. Fight this together because you'll have more power."

But Squeaky was a victim of a divide-and-conquer strategy. I believe others around him played on his weaknesses. They wanted him on their side so he wouldn't fight the will when it was contested. I can hear them say, "Come with us. We'll take care of you. Just don't go along with Gregory and contest the will."

It was the combined stress of being torn between two factions of the family that finally overwhelmed him, according to my mother. Squeaky got upset and slapped her.

This is what was happening to our family over my father's money. Instead of doing the right thing and taking care of his sons, the heirs under the will, members of the family succumbed to greed and engaged in a divide-and-conquer strategy.

Heading Out to the Cemetery

After the memorial we all got into these limousines and went out to the cemetery. I was in one limo with my wife and my children. It was kind of a cold and cloudy September day.

During the ride out there I remained in a state of disbelief that Miles was dead. I was hoping it was all a dream and that I'd wake up, but inside I knew that everything was real.

When we got to the cemetery I stood there and watched them place Miles into his marble mausoleum, wondering how our family was going to cope with this loss of someone who was so important to us.

I was thinking about how my father had given me a lot of love and guarded me during those early years of my life when I was helpless. In my mind I was praising him for that—even though he had turned out bad later in life with his Dr. Jekyll and Mr. Hyde personality.

Regardless of my father's behavior, I had nonetheless always tried to honor both my parents, although I wasn't always successful at doing so. I'm sure I could've done better.

Still, I was glad that over the years I had done battle for Miles and, at times in certain situations, even risked my own life for him. Sure he had developed a twisted personality because of fame and drugs, but I still loved him because he was my father.

Stabbed in the Back

I didn't say anything negative to my family at the memorial or the cemetery about them not flying me in when Miles was in the hospital, because I gave them the benefit of the doubt.

I thought maybe he had died too quickly for them to send me the money or something like that. That's what I was saying in my head. I was trying to justify their behavior. I thought that they were sorry too about what had happened, so why bring it up?

I also wasn't too angry at them because the will hadn't yet been probated and I still had no idea that I and my younger brother had been left out of it. But now, of course, I feel much differently. After all the years, I no longer give them the benefit of the doubt.

I still remember that after the funeral we all went to lunch together. They used Miles's Jazz Horn music business credit card to pay for it. That was the name of the production company that my father's manager had set up.

So there I was sitting down at the table and eating with members of my family. It was all very, very insidious. I did not know at the time that there was a conspiracy against me. I never dreamed I would not get a penny—not one cent—from the estate and that later in life I'd have to fight legal battles to get money from his royalties. They got it all.

My mother was also there. She had come in for the funeral all the way from St. Louis. But she had no idea of what had transpired until after the will was probated.

I Finally Learn the Truth

Some days later a letter arrived in the mail from the lawyers for the estate. They wanted me to admit the will to probate—to sign off on it.

When I looked at the will, my heart sank. I just couldn't believe what I was seeing. Erin, my sister Cheryl, Vince, Dorothy, and Vernon were getting everything. And yet they had the audacity to ask me to sign off on it.

It was ridiculous. Laughable. Sad. Tragic. Disgusting. Most of all, I felt furious! At the same time I was also feeling hurt that my family would do this to me. I partially blamed my father for all of this, and I'll tell you why a bit later on.

Meanwhile, I continued to be in a state of shock. Was this Miles's wish—to see the son who had been with him through thick and thin left without a cent? I didn't think so then and I don't think so now. Not the man who Jo said had talked about me all the time he was in the hospital and wanted me to be there with him in his final days.

Something was very wrong. In my heart I just knew that Miles had left something for me. My father always had a present for me when I was a kid—even if it was a pair of shoes or a baseball mitt. He would get mad at me sometimes—that's for sure—but not stay mad.

I remembered how Miles and I played baseball together, went to Yankee games and boxing matches together. We also got in and out of scrapes together. Does this sound like a father who so disliked his son that he would not put him into his will?

That's why I always believed that when Miles finally did get around to writing his will, despite any disagreements we might have had over the years, I and my children would be taken care of.

Never in my wildest dreams did I believe this could happen.

CHAPTER TWENTY

It Ain't Necessarily So
(Porgy & Bess, Columbia, 1958)

Poisoning His Mind Against Me

URING THE YEARS WHEN HE WAS living in California, I didn't call my father. I guess we both decided that we needed a break from each other.
It wasn't because of any animosity between us; I just decided to take a break because every man deserves a life of his own without being at the beck and call of his father. I was always there for him if he wanted to call me—it was his choice. But I didn't want to continue the way things were in the past. In addition to raising my family I wanted to go tp college and get my degree. I wanted to try and straighten out my life—not his. I didn't want to be tied to his pants struggling all the time with him to make things right for him. I wasn't his father—I was his son. I needed his help. It was a hard thing for me to do—but I did it. You'd have to take a walk in my shoes to fully understand it.

I was worn out being his bodyguard, and I wanted to pursue my own goals in life. I wanted to become a psychotherapist—which I eventually accomplished. I even got my Master's degree from Long Island University.

I was also certain that no matter where he was or what he was doing, if my father needed me all he had to do was call and I'd be there for him as I always had.

Forces had conspired to keep me away from my father's bedside as he lay dying. Still, no matter what, death should bring families together—not tear them apart. But that's the way it was with this family.

I know without a doubt that the will that emerged after Miles died was not Miles's final wish. It was not my father's final wish to disinherit me and Little Miles—to reach out beyond the grave and hurt us.

If Miles had been strong enough, had confronted his mortality, that will would not have read the way it did. I know that Miles probably looked up at them from his deathbed and was thinking that at least his sister and my sister were there, and that they'd call me and bring me to him. I'll go to my grave believing that.

I also believe that my Uncle Vernon played a role in this plot. He was a very intelligent and creative man who loved to draw, sang in a gospel choir, and appreciated opera.

Although he did so much for me over the years—he even once gave me a '68 Thunderbird when we were living back in St. Louis—he didn't come to my aid. Instead, he chose to play a silent role in the plot. He was like some guy who is watching his friend rape a woman. When the two of them are arrested he tells the judge, "I didn't rape her. I just watched." This guy should rightly get the same amount of time as the rapist did. That's how Vernon was. He knew what was going on but just watched and said nothing. He remained silent.

It's a Lie That I Wasn't Available for My Father

I want to set the record straight about this, because so much has been written about it in books that I've read about my father's life. Certainly it's true that I wasn't with Miles much during the 1980s when he re-emerged from his "retirement" and moved out to Malibu.

But we were never "estranged," like some books say we were, or even "antagonistic" to each other.

I wasn't with my father because God wants you to have a life of your own, and I simply decided to do something besides being Miles's bodyguard and nurse all the time. I needed out from the large shadow Miles cast. I needed normalcy.

I had a wife and two babies, and I was in school pursuing an education while trying to take care of my family. I couldn't also be my father's nursemaid. I had finally managed to buy my family a house in Georgia, and after settling them in there I went back North and enrolled in Long Island University to pursue my psychology degree.

But regardless of where I was or what I was doing, I was always available for my father—on call for whatever he needed. Miles knew he could pick up the phone and I'd be there for him like I always was.

And I always knew what he was up to from talking to my mother. We might not be in touch, but we really were. I would check in with my mother to see how Miles was doing. I knew what was going on with him; I also made sure that she and he had my address or P.O. box and phone number in case he needed to call. He just chose not to do so. The family tried to stigmatize me—saying that I had abandoned my father. No way in a million years was that true. We had a special relationship whether together or apart, and always would.

What hurts is that nobody called me to tell me my father died until the last moment when Cheryl called. She said Miles had been in the hospital for two days. I couldn't afford to fly out on the spur of the moment and the next day he was dead. It was only when I spoke to Jo Gelbard that I got the full picture of just how serious things were with him. She was the one who told me that Miles was calling for me. I never got any of these details from my own so-called sister.

It's also completely untrue that I felt animosity towards my father. I didn't. Maybe in his drug-distorted mind he believed that, but it's not the way I felt. Miles always had a tendency to build things up or make things up, so you were never sure exactly where you stood with him.

The real truth is that I loved both my parents. I was taught that you're not even supposed to raise your voice to a parent, and I tried to live by that rule. Certainly, over the years I had some disagreements with Miles only because I saw him becoming selfish and hard-hearted. I grew frustrated trying to show him how he was acting towards people. I also couldn't take the way he ruined himself doing drugs. He had cocaine, women, and music—not God—in his life, and that bothered me as well. He had no plan. He had no spiritual anchor and so he would fly all over the place doing nothing more than indulging himself.

I couldn't stand seeing how he surrounded himself with people who were no good for him, but were just there to use him—especially those women who Miles believed were in love with him but were really only in love with his money and his drugs.

That's why we parted. I did so with no animosity towards Miles and with the expectation that he could count on me if it was an urgent matter. But I eventually said, "Let me get something done for myself." I met Carol, fell in love with her, and she became my wife. We had two children together but, unfortunately, things didn't work out. We had our differences and a couple of years later we separated.

I remember my father once saying: "I'm not gonna make a will right now, because I don't want anybody killin' me." He was always paranoid about that. Well, like a good fence that makes good neighbors, a good will might have kept the family from fighting over his property.

I said earlier that I partially blamed my father for all of this mess pertaining to the will. That's because Miles's problem was that he always expected other people to be there to do mundane things for him without his even asking.

One of his big weaknesses was always using other people to take care of mundane matters in his life—even personal ones. He would always delegate responsibilities to others when he should have been taking care of business himself, like staying in touch with his son.

But Miles was Miles, and he somehow expected either someone else to do that for him or for me to be in touch with him when he needed help. But I wasn't a mind reader and nobody around him really cared.

As his lawyer testified, Miles never read his will before signing it. My father could have changed his will years before he died, but he didn't do so. That was Miles! Always depending on other people to handle even the most intimate matters in his life. And now it was too late. My father was too sick to do anything.

I'm absolutely positive that toward the end his life—even before he was hospitalized—my father had no intention to hurt his sons.

But even now, in his final moments, Miles was leaving it to others to make things right for him although at this point in his life he didn't have much choice in the matter.

Why We're Still a Divided Family

It's been 16 years since my father died, and this whole affair still shocks me. It is hard for me to believe what happened. I never did anything intentionally to hurt anyone in my family. Although maybe we weren't very close, my sister, my aunt, and I never had any real problems between us. But they had turned into people I didn't even recognize. I was made an outsider.

In all these years never once did my sister or my aunt say to me, "Gregory, I'm gonna put this in trust for your children. Let them know that Miles wanted them to get a good education." I wish I could give my children the opportunities Miles gave me—some of which I may not have appreciated when I was young.

I guess that some people, when they get a lot of money, just don't give a damn.

That's why we're a divided family. When a family's relationship is based solely on money instead of love, it has an insidious effect and can destroy it—which is exactly what happened to us.

The bedrock of any family is love. Instead, it's been materialized. We've been a family who all the way back placed an emphasis on education. Miles went to Juilliard. But some of the grandchildren today can't even afford to go to college and the estate won't help them. The only way I made it possible for my kids to go to college is that I'm a veteran and they were able to get student loans.

I believe it should be set in stone that if, under normal circumstances, you're a son or daughter you should benefit from your parents and not be deprived of an inheritance by some lawyer or some judge. I was always there for him and I feel that because of that I should have benefited from him—particularly because I'm the first son.

Lawyers and judges were not in the bedroom when this child was conceived, and they weren't in the house when this child was being raised. No judge or lawyer should be able to deprive a child of his father's inheritance.

In a perfect world, Miles would have provided for me in his will. While I lost the will contest because I ran out of money to fight, as Miles's son, due to a loophole in the law, I was able to recapture—many years later—Miles's copyrights.

Gregory Runs Miles's Voodoo Down

As Lloyd Jassin, a New York entertainment attorney who helped me get back 25% of my father's estate, explained, "Congress and copyright law looks after widows and children." Even though I was overlooked in the will, I was able to assert my natural right to Miles's songs with Lloyd's help. Being a fighter, I was able to "bump" or remove my uncle, aunt, and cousin from Miles's will—at least as far as Miles's copyrights were concerned. I guess Congress wanted to keep some of the music in the immediate Davis family.

The people who wrote Miles's will, and control his copyrights, were bound to know that copyrights go to the next of kin, not assorted brothers, sisters, and nephews. They haven't made it easy for me, even with the law being on my side. Which brings me to a matter I want to set straight.

The estate is what Miles left. Not the people in his will. When the *New York Times* refers to Cheryl, Erin, Dorothy, Vernon, and Vince as the estate, they are wrong. As Miles's oldest son, I was able to take back my father's songs. We are all Miles's heirs. Some took under his will; others, like me, took according to the law, or copyright statute. Not everyone shares equally, but we are all in this together—all being looked after by Miles.

So what does this mean? Miles's songs eventually came to me and my siblings—not Vernon, Dorothy, and Vince, who are not, technically, next of kin. While I may have been overlooked, I fought the machine, and I eventually won. If you look at Miles's will, there is nothing there that says, "I wish to disinherit Gregory." Like in the Bible, copyright law says you can't disinherit a son. Like I said, Miles admired fighters. He also respected people who stood up for themselves. I know somewhere Miles is looking down, smiling, proud that I fought clean and won.

Why I Think I Was Left Out

I guess that's the million-dollar question you're all wondering about by now. Why, exactly, wasn't I in my father's will to begin with? The answer to that is a rather complex yet simple one to explain. I believe I was!

I will believe until the day I die that Miles never read the will he signed and that there was no link between what Miles signed and what was in his heart. Does it mean he didn't know what was in his will? Perhaps. When he was deposed for the will contest, Miles's lawyer said that as best he could remember, Miles never read the will.

The signing, which was done in Miles's Essex House apartment, took a matter of minutes, moments maybe. Peter Shukat, his trusted attorney and business manager, testified that it was never read aloud. Miles didn't even see the original until the day he signed it. You've got to remember that Miles was on the decline. He was on a witches' brew of insulin for his diabetes, prescription painkillers, and antibiotics.

I believe that Miles IV and me were originally included in Miles's will, but then, somewhere along the line, Miles changed his mind under the spell of Mr. Hyde, who had really gotten hold of him by now.

In the grip of that personality, my father—who was like a chameleon, changing from day to day so that you never knew if you were in or out with him—could have been thinking, "Well, I don't see Gregory around and Miles Junior (or Squeaky) had already hit me so let me leave them out of my will."

But that will—even if he thought that way—was written three years before he died. I know deep in my heart that this wasn't the case when it came to his final days. I know without a shadow of a doubt that my father would never intentionally overlook his first two sons. I know that we were always in his mind and in his heart. Sure he might have remembered the problems he had with Squeaky, or that I was having some problems of my own.

Maybe when I asked for help when I went back to school, that set him off. No matter, Miles didn't need an excuse to act the way he did. But that was no reason to throw away a child's future. There were no serious problems between us. There was no animosity on my part, just a desire to get on with my own life.

I wasn't making any progress changing his drug habit, and, at the same time, I felt that God wanted me to have a life of my own. I was tired of being his bodyguard—doing little silly stuff like running around town escorting him on his drug buys and putting my life on the line for him. So I took my own little "hiatus."

There's only one other reason I can possibly think of that might have made Miles want to leave us out. In his twisted thinking maybe he thought it would hurt my mother, who he felt bitterness towards because she had remarried.

Assuming Miles even knew he disinherited us, my father had three years to think about what he had done and to reconsider it. And I know that he cared. After all, look at what Jo said to me when I spoke to her: "Your father talks about you all the time. You should really be here."

Even if Miles did originally leave me and Squeaky out of the will for some Milesish reason when he first wrote it—although I really don't think he did so—I just know that in the end he changed his mind and wanted to put us back in but couldn't. I just know that he left a will mentioning my mother and all his children. He had a hard life, and I know that he would not do something that would leave us in hardship for the rest of our lives— he wasn't that cold.

No matter how crazy this man might have become after he achieved his notoriety—with his Dr. Jekyll and Mr. Hyde personality—we were still Davises. I know that Miles believed you had to help your children. That's how it had always been in our family.

My brother and I never did anything that was so terrible he would decide to reach out from the grave to hurt us. There was never a murder plot. I never touched him physically, and there's no language in the will, as is often the case if you wish to avoid a will contest, saying he was deliberately leaving us out.

There's one final reason why I know my father had a change of heart. There was a final message from him that was relayed to me by a good friend of my Uncle Vernon.

"Tell Gregory that I tried to wait on him."

Epilogue

MY FATHER BROUGHT SOME BEAUTY into this world musically, but he also had a tortured soul that affected him until his death.

I think he always sought the equilibrium of normalcy in his life but was never able to find it. He was just using up too much energy by burning the candle at both ends.

My father didn't have the everyday ability of relating to his children, even when it came to looking out for their best interests after he died. His energy and focus was all directed to his music and art, so Miles was used to having people do the everyday things for him and in the end they failed him.

I think that when Miles was on his deathbed, he had a chance to review his life, and the person he saw who was always beside him when the going got rough was me. My father might not have thought I was perfect—and I wasn't—but he certainly knew without a doubt that I was always there for him.

Today, I have my own band. It's called the Gregory Davis Legacy Band. I learned a lot about music from my father, and I owe him a lot for that. But this is my own thing. It's me, not Miles. He wouldn't have wanted me to imitate him, because my father respected independent thinking.

So if people who come to hear me play want to relate to me as the son of Miles Davis, let them do it, even though I'm tooting my own horn.

Also, thanks to the hard work of my attorney, Lloyd Jassin, I have clearly established that I'm Miles's legal heir. In fact, I'm now getting 25 percent of my father's copyrighted songs. I hope someday to also get my long overdue and fair share of my father's estate, and to have a role in tending to Miles's legacy, just like I tended to him when we were together.

I certainly appreciate the musical legacy that my father handed down to me. And I'm in love with the trumpet and music the way Miles was.

But I don't want to label what I play jazz, just as my father didn't want to stay stuck with one musical form. Like him, I'm in love with melody, and maybe some of what he had has rubbed off on me.

But you want to know something? If Miles was sitting in an audience today and listening to me play, afterwards he'd be critical. He'd be proud that I'm endeavoring to make something out of my life and had an education—because sometimes Miles thought me and my brother were more interested in the street life than accomplishing things—but when it came to my music, I know he'd be critical. For Miles, being good was never good enough.

Sometimes when I'm walking around the city and see a Miles Davis poster hanging in a store window, I start thinking about my father. It makes me angry that the last act of Miles's life turned out the way it did. It makes me angry that due to the fact that Miles did something stupid because of his Mr. Hyde state of mind or because there was a conspiracy going on, part of his family is suffering financially.

"Tell Gregory that I tried to wait on him." These were among my father's last words.

So when I walk by a store and I see a poster of my father hanging there, tears sometimes come into my eyes. I look at that poster and what I want to say in return is that I wish you had, Miles. We needed to talk because we loved each other, and then we both would have felt complete . . .

Acknowledgments

BESIDES MY IMMEDIATE FAMILY— especially my mother, who put aside writing her own account of her life with Miles—I leaned hard on a few other special people to help me with this book. They gave me encouragement, direction, information, anecdotes, and memories to supplement my own.

These wonderful people include: Clark Terry, my godfather and one of my father's best friends; Betty Carter, who often acted as an alternate mother to me and sometimes my entire family; and Lester Bowie, the great trumpeter/composer, who was always my father's friend and always mine.

Also: Dr. Robert Taylor, director-archivist of contemporary music at Ohio State University; Ray Ross, the legendary jazz photographer; Gordon Lynch, colloquial historian of African-American music; Francis Cheers and Barbara Brunson, my researchers and sounding boards; and my spiritual uncle, Tony Malzone, without whose prodding and harassment this book would never have been written.

Much lasting appreciation, of course, goes to my bulldog of an agent—Lloyd Jassin—who through thick and thin believed in this project and is a big Miles fan.

There were also a couple of able hands who helped me collect my thoughts, straighten out my words, and shape the direction of this book. These include Bruce Wright, who prior to becoming a judge served for many years as one of my father's attorneys, and the late Nizam Fatah, former musician, prominent figure in the civil rights movement who was the executive director of the Inner City Roundtable of Youth. He was a family friend and witness to many of the episodes related in this book.

A few other special people in my life I'd like to acknowledge are my precious Gwen Dunbar for her love and support before, during, and after the writing of this book; Vernon Mann; and one of my newfound brothers, Peter Bradley.

I also can't thank Wayne Smallwood enough for the important doors he opened for me.

Last but not least let me thank Lesley Sussman, who has written books on gospel music, country music, and contemporary Christian music, and who finally came around to lend his considerable talents to the subject of jazz. His help, support, and patience in getting me to tell a very difficult story puts him high on my list of lifelong friends. When I read the first draft of the manuscript I laughed and I cried and I knew that finally what I had wanted to say for so many years was said.

Index

Photo Credits

Miles Davis as a child of nine or ten. Courtesy of Anthony Barboza collection.

Dr. Miles Dewey Davis, father of Miles Davis. Courtesy of Gregory Davis.

Dr. Miles Dewey Davis playing with Joseph, Miles's half brother. Courtesy of Gregory Davis.

Miles, Dorothy Mae, Vernon, and "Mama-Cleo." Courtesy of Anthony Barboza collection.

Four boys. Courtesy of Anthony Barboza collection.

Miles and Irene, outside their high school, 1940s. Courtesy of Gregory Davis.

Irene Davis at her home. Early 1980s. Courtesy of Gregory Davis.

Gregory in uniform in 1966. Courtesy of Gregory Davis.

Miles Dewey Davis IV—"Squeaky." Courtesy of Gregory Davis.

Miles in front of one of his paintings, 1969. Copyright © Baron Wolman.

Miles and Betty Davis, 1969. Copyright © Baron Wolman.

Miles with his Ferrari 275GTB. Copyright © Baron Wolman.

Miles behind the wheel of his Ferrari. Copyright © Baron Wolman.

Gleason's Gym in New York City. Copyright © Baron Wolman.

Miles was always a sharp dresser. Copyright © Anthony Barboza/Anthony Barboza collection.

Miles performing in the early 1980s in New York City. Copyright © Bob Leafe/Frank White Photo Agency

Miles at home in Malibu. Copyright © Anthony Barboza/Anthony Barboza collection.

Miles Davis's last trumpet. Courtesy of Gregory Davis.

Gregory Davis. Copyright © Cristo Holloway/Clockwork Apple.

Gregory Davis and Cheryl Davis at the Hall of Fame induction ceremony. Copyright © Frank Micelotta/Getty Images.